The Conscious Manager

Zen for Decision Makers

Fred Phillips

ISBN: 1-58151-079-9

In Memory of Fumio Toyoda

Acknowledgements

I thank all my aikido teachers, including Koichi Tohei, Rod Kobayashi, Bill Lee, and especially my sensei for the past twenty-five years, Fumio Toyoda. My mentors in business and education, Abe Charnes, Bill Cooper, George Kozmetsky, and Dave Learner, have my deep gratitude. They would all agree that while it's wise to choose excellent teachers, the successful student must bring something of himself to the task of learning – meaning that any mistakes and fatuities in this book are my own fault.

My family has supported my growth, and often tested it! Sometimes it's been a case of the wife and kids raising the dad.

My peers and friends in business, education, and Zen martial art have freely given me their support, and accepted support from me. I want them to know it's made all the difference.

The students who have kindly taken the time to tell me how I've influenced them, helped them, or changed their lives have touched me deeply.

The Conscious Manager also benefited from conversations with George Leonard, who was gracious and patient with this earnest writer. Professor Tom Roehl of Western Washington University kindly confirmed some facts about current business and financial practices in Japan, as did Howard Curtis (then of MCC in Austin) on Japanese language matters, and Professor Bruce Scott of the Harvard Business School on the history of globalization. Others who contributed to the effort via enlightening conversation or reviewing the manuscript include Julian Gresser, Scott Prahl, Alvin Tong, and Ginny Whitelaw.

The Conscious Manager

Contents

Beginnings

The light of consciousness embraces the whole universe.
    -Pan-Shan

"Wear a lot of hats?" complained the over-tasked manager, "I have to wear a lot of *faces*. And I hate it. I wish I could be the same person at work, at home, and with friends. I want my life to be all one piece, not a lot of fragments working against each other. Isn't that what integrity means? How can I make choices and decisions without feeling torn?"

This manager is expressing both emotional stress and spiritual hunger. If he fails to act on his hunger, he will feel frustrated. But if he expresses it, in words like those above, and acts upon it, then his spiritual hunger is a good thing! It is the first stage on the path of the conscious manager. This long and sometimes difficult path leads to the ability to make effective decisions with complete integrity.

The first section of *The Conscious Manager* is for the hungry manager. It provides a basis, a strategy, and useful tools for moving on to the later stages of the path.

1

To achieve a certain kind of thing, you have to become a certain kind of person. But then you will no longer be attached to that thing.
- Eihei Dogen (1200-1253)

Introduction

Fourteen years ago, I left my job as vice president of an old and well-known market research firm to teach in the MBA program at the University of Texas at Austin. Trained in the quantitative disciplines of Operations Research, I was caught short by my own first lecture on W. Edwards Deming's principles of quality. Only about five of Deming's fourteen principles, I realized, have anything to do with statistical quality control or other matters of an objective nature. The others have to do with the quality of the people in an organization. I mentioned to my dean that I'd been uncomfortable with the students' questions about this – I was, after all, their Operations Research professor and not their clergyman – so who was I to tell them what kind of people they should be? Don't worry, he told me, if you have something to teach, teach it.

Why of course! After all, I had then spent more than fifteen years of evenings training in and teaching Zen martial art – a discipline that places total emphasis on what kind of person you must be – and putting it aside each morning for my day job as scientist/executive. The dean had handed me a way to end my double life and to conduct myself in a unified way. (If you were to tell me I should have thought of it myself, you would be right, but such is the process of maturation.)

The MBA students warmed to my new approach. Social change in the last decades has resulted in reduced roles for family, religion and other traditional transmitters of values. Furthermore, in the fast-growth, high-tech companies that employ my current students, cultural values are still "under construction." MBA students who have had industry experience are trying to formulate values for their lives and find meaning in their work. Students with engineering backgrounds who have not undergone extensive socialization earlier in life have a particularly hard time getting along, much less exercising leadership, in a technology company where the cultural matrix is still unformed. They come to graduate school hungry to learn how to manage people, how to deal with the multinational knowledge workforce, and how to formulate ethical standards. MBA programs can serve by educating the whole person. Students appreciate class content that aids this process.

To live life all in one piece is a gift not easily gained. I cannot, now, imagine what my life would be like without the values I have learned from Zen martial art. How can one integrate these values – physicality, the reality of life and death, the imperative for sincerity and generosity – with the suit-and-tie pursuit of advantage in the business and political worlds? This book offers answers to this as well as to the more superficial question "How can skills from Zen martial art help one succeed in business?"

Both Zen and aikido (the martial art I practice) come from Asia. I spent time in Japan in my student days and later as a teacher. So the book is a double yin-and-yang, traveling back and forth between ideas from the East and from the West, and between looks inward at ourselves and outward at the commercial and political worlds.

The chapters use some Japanese terms, but meanings should be clear, and there is a glossary at the end of the book. While I anticipate that many readers will be martial arts students, I've taken pains to ensure all the ideas and terms are accessible to the majority who are not.

In fact, this book is for executives and managers. But anyone who wants to take responsibility and act effectively in business life and private life will enjoy reading it.

This book will help you see, and accept, the logical and emotional consequences of your life's goals and values. It will show you that it is possible to carry those values, without compromise, from your personal life into your corporate and political roles. It will show you, by means of examples from the U.S. and Japan, how to act on those values with integrity, in order to make responsible choices in your private life, in organizational decision making, and public policy.

Because this book brings Zen principles to bear on decision-making, you will find powerful and unusual points of view in these pages, and new ways to look at management. Perhaps these will spur you to train in Zen or aikido. They will, in any case, enable you to be a better manager.

As a graduate student with about three years of judo and aikido experience, I went to Japan in 1975-76. I had been given a United Nations fellowship to study economics in that country. Not yet understanding that life is all one piece, I felt guilty about spending most of my time sightseeing, meditating in a Zen temple, and training in aikido.

Subsequent years in the market research industry gave me little opportunity to revisit the Far East, but did afford the chance to consult for the U.S. Army Recruiting Command and the Assistant Secretary of Defense on the recruiting issues discussed in the chapter titled "Mind of the Warrior."

Shortly after I re-entered academe, Senator Jeff Bingaman of New Mexico decided there were too few technologists in the U.S. with Japan competence, and persuaded Congress to fund a grant program under the Air Force Office of Scientific Research (AFOSR) for university centers for the study of Japanese technology management. As if to confirm the Senator's premise, the best the enormous University of Texas could find to lead its AFOSR program was the likes of me, who had spent less than a year in Japan nearly two decades earlier and whose grasp of the language was rudimentary. Notwithstanding, the program produced successful educational activities and publications in the early 1990s, and together with the other AFOSR-supported universities, secured over a thousand internships in Japanese companies for American students.

Later, the offer to start a new graduate school of management in Oregon's "Silicon Forest" was irresistible. My move to Oregon informed some of the opinions in this book's discussion of environmental and "right to die" issues in which Oregon leads the other states. I have enjoyed directing the master's degree program in Management in Science and Technology at Oregon Graduate Institute (OGI, now a part of Oregon Health & Science University), and teaching its talented and experienced participants. With Scott Prahl, I have headed the OGI Aikido Club.

My aikido qualifications include 5th-degree rank and twenty-five years as an instructor. I have practiced Zen meditation as a layman for an equal number of years. Zen does thoroughly inform aikido practice, especially in the Aikido Association of America, to which the OGI club and I belong. But its formal practices and accreditation procedures are conducted by separate organizations.

There have been Zen books that told you how to get along with obnoxious co-workers, how to plan your career, and how to maintain your motorcycle. There are Zen books on how to cope with oppressive bosses.

But now you *are* the boss. You make decisions for yourself, your family, your company, your clubs and charities, and on political issues. You want to make these decisions responsibly, with integrity and good humor, and based on a positive and consistent set of values.

This book will help you do that.

Zen claims to be Buddhism, but all the Buddhist teachings are propounded in the sutras, and sutras are treated by Zen as mere waste paper, whose utility consists in wiping off the dirt of intellect and nothing more.
- D.T. Suzuki

Even before I can say it, it is no more.
- Sengai

How To Use This Book

What path teaches a manager to make decisions with responsibility, integrity and good humor? In this book we will call it the Zen way, or the master path. Others might call it a path of discipline or spirituality. Regardless of what road is taken, or what it is called, the way stations are the same. They are: Beginning (Hunger), Practice, Opening Experience, Support, Test, and Mission.

Whether in martial art or in management, the path begins with a hunger or longing for a better way, a dissatisfaction with the status quo. The student (from now on we'll call him or her the "manager") casts about for a practice or a teacher, and sooner or later experiences a psychological event of great intensity, opening her consciousness to wider possibilities. (Sometimes the opening event happens before the practice starts.) The manager finds a community of people on the same path, offering mutual support. A number of tests, scheduled and unexpected, formal and informal, help the manager advance on the path, and confirm or invalidate the practice. Finally, the manager chooses a mission to which he will apply his new skills effectively and without interference from ego.

The next-to-final chapter in the book is called "How To Become a Conscious Manager." It goes into more detail about these way stations. The earlier parts of the book are structured in sections named after each of the way stations. Following the introductory chapters, the specific practices of Zen and aikido are introduced, and two more chapters give tips that will enhance any master practice. Two chapters are devoted to the opening experience, providing examples of how a manager may open herself to new fields of compassion and perception. A section on support steers the reader to a number of books that reinforce a practice.

Tests and missions can come in many forms. The sections on these way stations let you consider missions that other people have adopted, and some current issues that demand conscious decisions and make good tests for all of us. Your own tests will be different, and if the business and social issues presented in these chapters are not the ones that move you, you may still take away the sense of how a conscious manager is tested.

The final chapters distill all these lessons into a step-by-step recipe for becoming a conscious manager.

The chapters parallel the steps of the path. You do not, however, have to read the chapters in order. Completing the path may take many years, versus only a few hours to read the book. You may want to refer to the book again when you have reached a later stage of your path.

Readers who have not practiced martial art or zazen should bring an open mind to the book's analogies between martial art and management. They are more apt than one might think. Airline executives must think about how flight crews can handle incidents of "air rage" and subdue fractious passengers without endangering others and without courting lawsuits. Those who run controversial organizations, for example, agencies that draw protests because of environmental, labor, family planning or globalization issues, must have policies and training programs that deal with physical confrontation. One chapter of this book deals with the World Trade Organization's 1999 ministerial conference, where police over-reaction to protests left WTO and the city of Seattle, as well as the protesters, with black eyes.

The Zen path is a highly individual experience, and so the book does not prescribe too specifically. But to bring the book's general discussions down to earth, most chapters feature a Management Challenge. This is a vignette based on characters like the people you and I work with. They are facing situations that bring home the theme of the chapter. The resolution of the situation (if there is one) depends on exercising the characteristics of a conscious manager. It is a challenge not just for the protagonist, but also for you, the reader, who must ask yourself how you would act in that situation.

Some chapters also include physical or mental exercises you can do on your own, or with a partner, to better understand what it means to be a conscious manager. Don't be embarrassed to try them!

Several chapters also conclude with a take-away tool that you may use right away to improve your decision making.

Another feature of the book is the occasional Question-and-Answer. I admit to making up a few of the questions, but most are real questions from students, friends, and colleagues. One of my aikido peers sent me this question:

Q My favorite comment on Zen was given to me by my teacher when I asked him, "Sensei...what is Zen?" After a long pause, eye contact, and a smile, he replied, "If I say.... it's not Zen."

Yes, any time you freeze reality in black and white words, it's no longer Zen. Many fine Zen books have been written before this one. Their pages have inspired readers, wrapped sandwiches, and lined kitty litter boxes. May this book, also, serve you well!

Now here is a more serious way to answer your question. The highway sign pointing to Detroit is not itself Detroit. This book is not Zen, but it is a pointer. Like the highway sign, it might help you slow down, and turn in the direction you already want to go.

Samurai during [Japan's] warring stage were in daily contact
with questions of life and death, of intention and concentration.
They saw in the meditative discipline of monks a kind of dynamic
calm and courage that they needed as soldiers. Monks, also, saw
in the warriors the same intense energy and single-minded
commitment that was necessary for their own spiritual training.
Through their interchange, the martial arts in time became viewed
as potential tools for spiritual development; they became known
as Budo, martial ways.
- Fumio Toyoda

Everything the same; everything distinct.
- Zen proverb

Zen, Martial Art, and Management

Zen stems from Buddhism, and is the essential core of that tradition. It is important for readers to understand that this book is not about religion or proselytizing. Those who think of a religion as a system of beliefs should know that Zen encourages no beliefs whatsoever, and in fact holds that any beliefs or fixed ideas clog up the free-flowing process of enlightenment through interaction with the world. Despite this, as we shall see, the practice of Zen should lead to very moral behavior.

Buddhism is based on "four noble truths." These explain that human suffering is due to our attachment to attained, unattained, and unattainable things, and that suffering can be alleviated by overcoming these attachments. Guidance on how to do this is given in the "eightfold path," which advises on thought, action, meditation, and compassion. These were realized and taught by Gautama Siddhartha, called the Buddha. Buddha means "the one who woke up" (hence the title of this book), or "enlightened one." Cutting away attachments does not turn one into an unfeeling robot. On the contrary, because the ego is an imaginary wall between our "individuality" and our fellow humans, loosing the attachment to one's own ego enables a more selfless love for others. Advanced practitioners of Zen may have attachments, but these are deliberate and not compulsive.

Buddha's teaching was in no way warlike, and in many ways pacifistic. Yet its connection to martial art, centuries later, was logical, as is its connection to business today. Martial analogies serve the conscious manager well when he focuses on war's imperative for strategic action, instantaneous response, and dealing with fear and compassion. However, war is destructive and tragic.

Business and politics can involve "creative destruction" that sweeps aside the old in favor of the new, but business and politics also *con*struct wonderful new products, organizations and institutions.

Analogies that focus only on the destructive aspects of war and management fail. In fact, we know something is seriously wrong when a company's president (as actually happened in one firm known for indiscriminate downsizing) earns the nickname "Chainsaw." U.S. President Richard Nixon was fond of brutal, unsubtle analogies between politics and football. Perhaps it is not surprising that Nixon is remembered mostly for illegal acts, offensive utterances, and thuggish associates.

☯

Almost everyone has some friends or colleagues who seem driven by career goals that are not really making them happy. Thus, the idea that attachment is the source of discontent is plausible. That meditation is the antidote to attachment might be harder to accept. Yet both statements are true.

The principle is simple. Toyoda's words show, however, that Zen is a hard, demanding path. A rich Zen psychology diagnoses the common obstacles and, often through parables, offers guidance. The parables pull no punches; usually they are anything but comforting. As conscious managers, we must face disturbing issues. The cold, clear psychology of Zen helps us avoid the denial, ego-stroking, and euphemisms that do nothing to help solve a problem.

As conscious managers, then, we work on becoming aware of our attachments. In this way we are able to overcome them – including our attachment to ego, and our clinging to the very idea of seeking enlightenment. We are already enlightened, after all. It is only our attachment to distracting irrelevancies that prevents us from understanding this, and prevents us from consistently taking enlightened action.

Generally speaking, this means the conscious manager...

... attends to detail but looks at context; tries to see the big picture.

... doesn't believe everything he or she is told.

... rejects easy labels.

... constantly hones personal skills.

... is committed to lifelong learning – for everyone in the organization.

... exercises respect and compassion, but not indulgence, in all dealings.

... is flexible but not wishy-washy.

... spares no effort to match the right people with the right jobs.

... lets employees put their best foot forward.

... controls the organization loosely.

...gives employees the chance to stretch themselves.

... tries to see the adversary's point of view.

... shows a creative imagination.

...is focused and steadfast in pursuit of a mission.

...uses every tool at his or her command.

How can a manager become aware of attachments? Through meditation, through mindful practice, through the support of other students of conscious management, through challenges and tests, and through instruction from a qualified, compatible teacher. This book will provide guidance and clues about each of these.

The discussion above makes reference to "mission." Our first Management Challenge illustrates what this means.

Management Challenge: A mission and its pursuit. Dan tells everyone his dual missions in life are democracy in Russia and better education in the U.S. Deciding on that mission – and repeating it to himself and others – helps him focus, makes him more effective, and attracts people who can help further the mission. Dan has decided these are the issues on which he wishes to make a difference.

A family crisis looms just as Dan is planning an important testimony to Congress. What should Dan do?

Dan knows the usual limits of what one man can do. He knows neglecting his family in order to advance political and educational goals will lead to more unhappiness rather than less, so he makes sure he attends to family matters before mission matters. He cancels the testimony, and luckily the family crisis turns out to be minor. His family understands he has sacrificed an important opportunity to bring an issue to Congress' attention, and they are now even more supportive of his policy-related efforts. For his own part, Dan doesn't dwell on the fact that this minor crisis needn't have kept him from Washington on that day. He moves on.

Slow progress on his goals won't crush his ego; Dan pursues his mission with an admirable mix of passion and detachment. He is a conscious manager.

Buddhist tradition features the Bodhisattva character, an enlightened individual who, realizing the futility of grasping at the world, nonetheless does not abandon the world. Compassion, without attachment, motivates the Bodhisattva to commit to helping others reach enlightenment. This is the Bodhisattva's mission.

A manager's duty to the development of employees is similar. When an organization has conscious managers at all levels, paying attention to detail in the best Zen manner, they will almost always find that "if you take care of the little things, the big things will take care of themselves."

It is easy for Western business people to embrace the concept of mission, because every business plan has a mission statement. It is more challenging to understand the difference between single-mindedness and attachment. A business mission must be pursued single-mindedly, but written between the lines of the business plan is the implied threat, "If this doesn't work, we're all done for." When we stop believing that threat – when we cut our attachment to it and to the fears it engenders – we are on the way to enlightenment and more effective execution of the mission.

☯

By now, the joke about the cheap Zen vacuum cleaner – it comes with no attachments! – is well known. The joke is a light-hearted reminder that non-attachment is one of the most powerful and useful ideas in the history of philosophy. To the conscious manager, non-attachment is more than an idea. It is a guiding principle and a way of life.

☯

Q Fred, there are Zen masters who were tyrannical with their disciplesand held the reins of their organizations tightly. So can Zen lead to conscious management? I think some of your other tenets could bear strengthening too: "Rejecting easy labels" should read "rejecting all labels." "Tries to see the big picture" might better be "sees the big picture," and "Doesn't believe everything he or she is told" should be replaced by "believes nothing."

Commitment to lifelong learning seems hard to justify in terms of Zen. Perhaps your book explains how lifelong learning is justified by a philosophy that advocates sitting for long periods of time. Learning leads away from the path of enlightenment, doesn't it?

A You are right on target. This book talks about not believing anything at all, but it is inefficient in management to reconfirm everything you read or hear. We tend to assign levels of reliability to different information sources. The main thing is to be aware that we are playing the probabilities, and not to grasp at certainties that do not exist.

As you continue your practice of mindfulness, your awareness grows, and you become aware of more things and more interactions. The result is "getting the big picture" more often. You may not wish to call this kind of cognitive change "learning," but you'd be nitpicking.

Most of us manage in a way that is too controlling. We need to learn to manage loosely. Like aikido techniques, however, management involves a yin and yang, a time for letting things happen and a time to forcefully assert influence.

Shihan Toyoda notes that medieval Japan was fertile ground for the growth of Zen. Many schools sprouted up, with different kinds of abbots. The diversity of approaches was part of the vitality of the culture of that time. Taoist scholar Alan Watts mentions that this was the first time and place (except for a couple of short-lived earlier instances in China) that it was possible and necessary to train large numbers of young monks at one time. Two aspects of this required managerial skill: Handling the large numbers of students, and influencing Japanese society to maintain itself as a cordial environment for the transmission of Zen. Like organisms and their ecological niches, Watts says, Zen and Japanese society co-evolved. Today in the U.S., we face similar issues of the co-evolution of society and our businesses, and the transmission of our preferred way of management, i.e., being conscious managers. Co-evolution is a fancy way of saying "lobbying, public relations, advertising and politicking," along with teaching and mentoring. It's not always "pure" in an idealized sense, but it is still Zen. Zen does not idealize.

Practice

Enlightenment comes from practice;
Thus enlightenment is limitless.
Practice comes from enlightenment;
Thus practice has no beginning.
-Dogen

A regular practice that concentrates the mind, and in which the movements of the body become second nature, frees the mind for creative enlightenment. Practicing a master path with a proven tradition, a manager is more likely to have the opening experience that is an essential step toward conscious management.

Even when the manager has learned who he is, regular practice helps *remind* him who he is.

Having recognized his hunger for a better way, our manager must act on it. The best action is a practice.

All the troubles of man come from his not knowing how to sit still.
- Blaise Pascal

There is no other way but to meditate.
- Sir Francis Bacon

A Primer on Zazen

Zazen – What and Why?

Zazen is intensive, formal sitting. Although it may sound boring, if you try zazen, you will find it is both difficult and interesting. Experienced practitioners say they sit because they sit; they have no attachment to outcomes or results. You may feel that way too, eventually. In the meantime, don't be ashamed to practice zazen for self-improvement. Early payoffs are almost guaranteed. If you later decide to adopt zazen as a way of life, fine. If not, that's okay too.

Zazen will improve your performance in athletics or martial art, and your concentration and effectiveness at work. It is an effective tool for relaxation. As you practice, you will deal with people and complex situations in new and better ways. Practice still more, and you will find a new balance in your life.

People from all philosophical and religious backgrounds sit zazen, which stems from Zen Buddhist tradition. While no preaching or proselytizing is involved in zazen, I won't pretend that sitting will never challenge your beliefs. If you are secure in your home tradition, and don't mind some challenges to your ego, you and zazen will go together like fish and chips.

Exercise: *Working up to zazen.* Sit on one or more cushions that you have placed on a soft rug or mat. Adjust the number of cushions so you can sit up straight without undue discomfort. You may sit in "full lotus" (each outside ankle resting on the opposite thigh), half lotus (one ankle on the rug and the other resting on your thigh), or simply cross-legged with both ankles on the rug. Rest your hands on your thighs.

Your aim in the first exercise is just to sit still for five minutes. You may think about anything (food, girlfriend, boyfriend, kids, work) or about nothing at all. But *don't move.*

If you get an itch, don't scratch. If you become uncomfortable or feel some pain, don't squirm. You'll only have to withstand it for five minutes! Notice whether the itch or pain persists or goes away by itself.

Repeat this exercise once or twice a day for as many days as you wish before reading the more advanced instruction below. While you are not yet doing true zazen, you have begun to travel a valuable path: You are playing with your consciousness, in a safe, drug-free way. You are learning to slow down, to be less reactive to minor irritations, to distinguish perceived threats from real threats, and to observe how your body and mind react to all this.

And if you don't play with your consciousness, how can you find out who you are?

Mind

You may have read that zazen is "no-mind" *(mushin),* and also that meditation is a "mindful path." How you can set your mind to achieving no-mind? Does the seeming contradiction of mindfulness and no-mind turn you against the idea of meditating?

When people say meditation, they usually mean contemplation. That is, contemplating a work of art, the grandeur and mystery of the universe, or one's navel. Zazen is not contemplation! And so, zazen is not meditation. It is not even "introspection." Do you remember the poster from the 1960s that said, "Sometimes I sits and thinks, and sometimes I just sits"? Zazen is *just sitting.* You'll find that awareness (perhaps a more fitting word than mindfulness, as it doesn't suggest self-consciousness) will grow from just sitting.

Despite what you've heard about contemplating nothingness, zazen is something else. It is less than contemplation, and more. Naturally, thinking about nothing is different from not thinking about anything. As you become experienced with zazen, you will find yourself not thinking about anything, but that is never forced. Some parents cruelly punish their child's misbehavior by telling him or her to stand in the corner and "don't think about elephants." Imagine the child's guilt at being unable to keep from visualizing elephants! Zazen is not punishment. No teacher will tell you not to think about anything. We can just predict – based on the cumulative evidence of thousands of person-years of zazen practice – that eventually you will experience not thinking about anything. This aspect of mushin – accepting sensory input without judging, classifying, analyzing, arguing, over-reacting, attaching, or getting distracted – is an important part of your training. It is also a liberating feeling and a powerful tool for seeing your attachments clearly, and for quickly cutting to the essence of a decision situation.

In the meantime, as you sit, thoughts will come and go. Let them come and go. If you have enough self-discipline to begin zazen, you will not let your thoughts carry you away. Thoughts have no mass, and unless put into action, no force. So how can they carry you away? When you realize they cannot, you have begun to develop the *center* that the twentieth-century Zen master Shunryu Suzuki likened to a swinging door that remains in one place while letting thoughts pass.

Guilt about your thoughts is pointless. There is harm only when you are the prisoner of your destructive thoughts. By cultivating your swinging door, you can make sure you are never the slave of your thoughts.

Some zazen practitioners like to count their breaths as a way of calming body and mind. Do this as long as it helps you; abandon it when it doesn't help you any longer. Remember that counting to large numbers keeps higher rational centers of the brain active, and also tempts you to set irrelevant goals, like "I will sit for 150 breaths." To avoid these effects, count up to five breaths, then start over each time you reach five.

Body

Don't drive yourself crazy by constantly checking these minutiae about posture. Be aware of them, and if your posture feels wrong, mentally run down the list to figure out how to correct it.

The pyramid. Imagine a triangle with corners near your knees and behind your tailbone. Your "one-point" (the point in the lower abdomen about four finger widths below the navel) will be the apex of a pyramid whose base is that triangle. Your awareness will be centered at this point, even though the paragraphs below point out the ways other parts of your body contribute to a good zazen posture.

Weight forward of sit-bones. When you sit cross-legged, you can feel, where the femurs meet the pelvis, two bony protrusions pressing against the floor. These are the "sit-bones" (ischia), and when you sit zazen your weight should be forward of the sit-bones. If you try setting your weight behind the sit-bones, you'll see that it is difficult to keep your spine upright.

Hands. Lightly grasp your left thumb with the fingers of your right hand. Fold your left fingers around the back of your right hand. Rest your joined hands in your lap with the palms turned upward.

Lining up the "third eye" and one-point. The point between your eyes and just above your eyebrows should be vertically above your one-point. As you sit, these two points tend to become one in your perception. But the vertical alignment cannot happen unless you tuck in your chin, and most beginners don't "tuck" correctly.

Tucking the chin in. If you simply tilt the point of your chin toward your Adam's apple, you will tip your spine forward, ruining your posture and creating tension in your upper back. Instead, keeping your shoulders immobile, move your whole head backward as if your ears were on horizontal tracks. Comfortably elongate your spine. Forehead and one-point are now aligned. Your chin is also closer to your Adam's apple.

Stretching the spine. To achieve a good zazen posture, the spine must be upright and stretched. When you first sit down, you might wish to imagine a string pulling the crown of your head upward. Your spine needs to be pulled at both ends if it is to be elongated, and so you will "set the hara." To set hara, curl the lower end of your spine forward just a bit.

In martial art, we emphasize centering mentally at the hara or "one-point," a spot in the lower abdomen, to optimize balance and power. In zazen you can't just forget about one-point and get preoccupied with your tail and the top of your head! Check your posture, of course, but in the end your attention must rest in the lower abdomen. The phrase "setting hara" reinforces this, calling attention to hara even though what you're really doing is adjusting your tailbone. I recommend taking yoga classes so you will develop the habit of elongating your spine. Then in zazen, you will do this naturally without having to think about it too much.

Looking at the ground "six feet in front." This is classic zazen instruction, but you may find that looking downward at this angle causes a slump in your posture. If so, look at a spot farther forward. If there is another row of students sitting in a facing row, do not look directly at any individual. This would distract both of you.

When you start to slump, adjust. Muscles tire, and your posture changes over the course of a long sit, without your volition. Staying in a bad posture for the remainder of the sit won't help you or others, so you may readjust. When you are in a group, it is of utmost importance not to disturb the concentration of your fellows. So readjust your posture slowly and smoothly – no squirming!

Integrating

I like the description of zazen as "calm expectancy." When we expect something important to happen in the next few seconds, we don't start any complicated thought processes. We wait with an empty mind. At rest, but ready for anything, our minds and bodies are efficient and flexible.

If you're a Westerner, your own religious tradition may include waiting for the Messiah. I might suggest, without intending disrespect, that these traditions have not dealt too well with reputed arrivals of actual messiahs. We're all better at waiting. Indeed, it is the waiting that is the important thing. The awaited event might happen in a hundred years, or next Tuesday, but then again, it might happen any moment!

Zazen makes waiting into a science. A Zen injunction says, "Sit as if your hair were on fire." Zen emphasizes good sense, so if your hair were on fire, I hope you would get up and put it out. It's a metaphor, of course. If your hair were on fire, it would focus your concentration wonderfully. So when you sit, pay attention fiercely. What's fierce about sitting in calm expectancy? Only the sharp-edged focus of your concentration.

Q In this chapter you asked, "If you don't play with your consciousness, how can you find out who you are?" Well then, if I *do* play with my consciousness, or sit zazen or whatever, how does that help me find out who I am?

A Isn't it odd that the English word "business" literally means busy-ness, and doesn't seem to imply anything about making good products, making a profit, or building a lasting enterprise? It stems from the Puritan notion that the idle mind is Satan's playground. In any case, plenty of people cannot stand to be idle. They always have to be doing something. Indeed, they define their identity in terms of *doing*. When they spend a quiet day by a river, they call it fishing – even if they will be happier not to catch any fish!

Other people define themselves by what they experience. Sensory input is essential to their identity. The radio is always on, or the TV. Entertainment must be a movie, a performance, or an exhibit.

Zazen, obviously, takes us away from the doing and experiencing modes, and causes us to examine how central these things really are to our identity.

Artists define themselves by their creations. Neurotics by the little bundle of tensions they assemble for themselves each morning. Hypochondriacs define identity in terms of their ailments, always pleased to give an "organ recital" should you be so foolish as to inquire about their health. Still others define themselves by their family relationships, their hometown, or their tribal affiliation.

Zazen is an experience all our own, that returns us to the well of creativity, lets us drop our tensions, and improves our health. Only you can know what is essential to your selfhood. As you cannot recognize the essential while you cling to the non-essentials – your tensions and pretensions – a path of non-attachment is the best way to find out who you are.

Sitting zazen may lead you to the point of view that you are, at bottom, a *point of view*. In Mexico, you can buy a ten-inch square construction of sticks and yarn called an "ojo de Diós," an eye of God. A person who is meditating, calmly observant, well-connected to the universe but with neither attachment nor aversion to doing, consuming, or creating may well be called an ojo de Diós. This, though, is whimsically poetic, and from a Zen perspective, just another idea to get past.

Freud categorized people as anal-retentive, oral-assimilative, and so on. In contrast, as we shall see in coming chapters, a Zen adept eats when hungry, shits when needful, and can pay full attention, with an attitude of acceptance and equanimity, to each.

A child psychologist once asked a variety of children to draw pictures of themselves. Suburban kids of European descent tended to fill up the paper with drawings of their faces. Navajo children, instead, drew a tiny human figure surrounded by outlines of mountain and desert scenery, animals and plants. These diverse views of identity are wonderful. Each is valid, and each is limiting.

Q Wait a minute. It's taken me all my life to put together the bundle of wants, needs, achievements, and tensions that are "me." I worked hard to build my ego, and I deserve to keep it.

A No. You are a human being, and you deserve more.

⊙ *Tool: Sit still.* The skill to sit quietly, disconnected (however briefly) from your usual sources of ego sustenance, should be your minimum take-away from this chapter. It is the start of deeper experiences of life and management.

'Tis the gift to be simple,
'tis the gift to be free;
'tis the gift to come down
where we ought to be.
And when we are in the place just right
we'll be in the valley of love and delight.

When true simplicity is gained,
to bow and to bend we will not be ashamed.
To turn, to turn will be our delight,
'till by turning, turning
we come 'round right.
- Shaker hymn

Aikido and the Conscious Manager

When attacked, a practitioner of the Japanese martial art of aikido bends, turns, bows, and, reaching just the right place, can send even a larger attacker flying through the air. Throws, joint locks, and take-downs are emphasized in this moving embodiment of Zen; defensive punches and kicks are rarely seen. In this, aikido resembles the older art of judo. Unlike judo, aikido is practiced strictly as defense. Therefore, there are no tournaments in aikido.

Aikido requires a clear mind, a relaxed body, and a calm acceptance of the attacker's energy. Acceptance means the aikidoist does not fight. Fighting and struggling are mindsets, creatures of the relative world. There are no struggles in the absolute world, only events. By cutting her attachment to the fighting mindset, the aikidoist preserves her safety and demonstrates compassion for her attacker, who is usually deposited on the ground without injury and with at most momentary pain. In the best of cases, the attacker's anger is dissipated, and friendship may result.

The aware, compassionate aikidoist has the skill to see a dangerous situation brewing and, sometimes, defuse it before it reaches the level of violence. Having reduced his attachment to ego, the martial artist can walk away from insults and threats, protecting the safety of attacker and defender without resorting to aikido throws. It is truer to say that *these* are "the best of cases." The physical techniques of aikido are actually a last resort, though even these throws and pins leave the door open for reconciliation with the attacker.

It will be fun to introduce the art with a presentation some fellow aikidoists and I gave to the Austin Opera Guild before the opening of *Madame*

Butterfly. Enter the auditorium, take your seat, listen to the narrative, and use your imagination...

[Narrative begins.]

Ross, Dan and David are showing you the unarmed techniques of the Japanese martial art called aikido. Let me call your attention to some of the things they are doing. Although the person attacking may do so by hitting or kicking, the defender does not respond in kind. Defense consists of controlling the attacker's wrist, arm, or body, leading to a throw or a takedown. Despite the dance-like appearance, this is effective self-defense. Yet the attacker, who is thrown, is not injured. Both attacker and defender are smiling and seem to be enjoying themselves. The defender remains relaxed through the entire process.

Ross is now demonstrating a formal exercise with the *bokken,* or wooden practice sword. The sword is an important symbol in Japanese culture, and the sword is also central to the practice of aikido.

As is true of so many other arts, sword-making came to Japan from the Asian mainland and in Japan was refined to its utmost level. For hundreds of years, Japanese sword-making has been a treasured cultural art. Although the sword I am holding is a replica, you can see that its design is beautiful as well as deadly. Please do not touch the blade. I assure you it's very sharp. Dan and Eric are showing us a two-person *bokken* exercise. Although this is a set piece, you can see that it demands total concentration and sensitivity to the opponent's intention.

In the West, we learn that Gordius, King of Phrygia, once tied a knot in a piece of rope. Many wise men tried and failed to unravel this knot, until Alexander the Great cut it in two with his sword. Ever since, the knot has symbolized a complex problem, and "cutting the Gordian knot" has symbolized bold decisiveness. The word "incision" means a cut. "Decision" means eliminating alternatives. The similarity of the words is no accident.

In Japan, it is recognized that the fundamental act of human cognition is to make a distinction. We say, "This is not that." But to distinguish a thing from all other things is to take a sword, figuratively, and cut the universe in two.

Thus the sword is associated with the ability to conceptualize, which is the one thing that separates humans from animals. A very deep symbol. No doubt this is why Mme. Butterfly did herself in with the blade, and not, say, a leap into Nagasaki Harbor.

Another adopted art that reached its pinnacle in Japan is the Buddhist practice of Zen. It is a great insight of Zen that our ability to conceptualize is a recent and imperfect graft onto our older, animal nature. Our animal nature reacts only to the moment. Our higher faculties allow us to learn and plan – but also to anguish over what might have been. We ease the conflict between our two natures by sitting Zazen. David is demonstrating the proper Zazen posture. If you remember the association of the sword with the conceptualizing self, you can understand why Zen and the martial arts have been closely tied throughout Oriental history. Quite aside from any quest for enlightenment, Zazen is very soothing, and its calming effect improves the student's performance in the martial arts and other endeavors.

In the West, we think of the sword as an instrument of destruction – what the Japanese call *satsujinken*. In the East, its association with Zen, and with consciousness itself, makes it possible to think of the sword as a means of protecting life. This is called *katsujinken*. In the year *Mme. Butterfly* is set, a Japanese man named Morihei Ueshiba was about twenty-two years old. Already an accomplished martial artist, he saw the need for a new art that could be used non-lethally and compassionately, in keeping with his religious ethics and with the rule of civil law that characterized Japan's Meiji Restoration. Ueshiba O-Sensei combined movements taken from the traditional sword arts of kenjutsu with modified unarmed jujitsu arts, to create a beautiful and non-destructive yet totally effective martial art, which he called *aikido*. As the students demonstrate, please notice the principle of blending. Each defense begins with acceptance of the attacker's intention. The defender moves to a position that is safe from follow-up attack; then harmonizes with the attacker's intended direction of motion; and only then takes the initiative that leads to a new equilibrium with the defender in control. You can see why many people have drawn an analogy between this principle of martial art and the Japanese economic strategy of the past few decades.

In 1976, I had the good fortune to visit Nagasaki. It is a lovely semitropical town, with high hills descending into the Sea of Japan. In the days of the Shoguns, all non-Japanese traders and missionaries visiting Japan had to reside on a small island in Nagasaki harbor so that Japanese society would not be "contaminated" by their influence. Much of Nagasaki's history as Japan's window to the West remains visible, including the home of the American Consul who appears as a character in *Madame Butterfly*. That history is now overshadowed by Nagasaki's most important role in human memory, as the second target of the atomic bomb. Relics of the explosion and its aftermath are preserved in Nagasaki. They are utterly moving and unforgettable. The photograph on the easel shows the monument erected at ground zero; a ruined building that was relocated to the park near the monument; the hills of Nagasaki in the background; and a neon sign that flashes "OK" with some irony.

I hope this demonstration has inspired you to begin the study of aikido. Thank you for your attention.

[End of narrative.]

Naturally, after the presentation, there is a Q&A session.

Q How do you say it?

A Eye, key, dough.

Q Does it require brain or brawn?

A Actually, neither. Aikido is beautifully designed to let every practitioner make the most of his or her strength. Intellectuals do seem drawn to aikido, perhaps because of its complexity and aesthetic. However, over-intellectualizing it slows down one's learning.

Q I've never done anything like it before, and I'm afraid the instructor will lose patience with me.

A I find it a joy to work with beginners. I believe most aikido instructors feel the same way.

Q Can teens participate? Can my nine year old son participate?

A Aikido does great things for the awkwardness and fragile self-esteem that seem to accompany the teen-age years. Many Aikido schools have classes just for children. In these classes, kids often master Aikido techniques faster than adults do.

Q What would I need?

A At first, just a good attitude and some sweats or gym shorts and T-shirt. Later, you'll want to buy a gi to wear.

Q Is it like tai ch'i or more geared toward marshal arts?

A Very much like tai ch'i in its emphasis on internal energy, but you start with pairs attack-defense practice right away in aikido, and there's a lot of falling down, getting up, falling down, getting up...

By the way, that's "martial" art. Reminds me of the yellow pages ad (this is true, and thank goodness it wasn't an aikido ad) where the guy promoted himself as "grandmaster world marital arts champion." Made me wonder whether it was the indoor or the outdoor championship.

Q Where does aikido came from and how does it compare to other martial arts?

A Aikido is from Japan. Its physical movements are descended from jujitsu and the Japanese sword arts. It differs from the martial arts you see on "Kung Fu Theater" in that the defensive arts are all throws and takedowns, not punches and kicks. I think aikido is more fun than most similar arts, and you learn physical/mental skills you can use in everyday situations other than self-defense.

Q I have taken tae kwon do for two years and attained a green belt. Will aikido fit in with my tae kwon do experience?

A You will probably find that aikido does not build directly on your tae kwon do experience. They are very different. Many long-time tae kwon do practitioners do train in aikido, either at the same time, or after discontinuing their TKD practice.

Q I had a knee injury...

A No one in my class is required to do anything they don't feel up to. Talk with an aikido instructor. Chances are the instructor will invite you to try some classes while you determine your comfort level.

Q Is it good for reducing stress? Relaxation? Can I burn a few calories?

A Great for stress reduction. You really won't get much aerobic exercise out of this until you feel confident about the basic movements, and that could take a few months.

Q What should I expect to learn?

A You will learn a healthful exercise that you will be able to practice all your life. (Aikido does not jolt your joints; you won't have to give it up when you turn forty). You will learn effective self-defense. You will learn stress control. You will learn ways of dealing with conflict that can carry over into work and family life.

Q What if I'm a web junkie?

A The Aikido Association of America is at http://www.aaa-aikido.com/The page of my dojo in Oregon is http://omlc.ogi.edu/aikido/. Aikido magazine sites include http://www.aikidojournal.com/ and http://www.aiki.com/. Find an aikido school near you at http://www.aiki.com/ or http://www.aikiweb.com/ .

Q What kinds of people practice?

A A delightful rainbow of people of all ages, genders, colors, and economic situations. Outside the United States and Japan, aikido is popular in Europe, Latin America, and the Middle East. My own university club students are mostly professionals and graduate students who gather to get some exercise in a structured but relaxed, friendly and noncompetitive atmosphere. Most are in their twenties or thirties, though a few are older or younger. Participants in their sixties are not unusual, and there are a few high school and college students among us. Few of us are superb athletes, but that doesn't stop us from trying physical things that are new to us. We believe we didn't stop learning when we left school. We have no use for fads and don't really feel we have anything to prove.

Q I don't much like what I've seen of martial art training...

A Perhaps you have always felt curious about the martial arts of the Far East, but have been put off by physically punishing regimens or by the aggressive attitude of many students and teachers of the martial arts. If your exposure to martial art in America has been limited to full-contact karate or Sunday afternoon kung-fu theater, or if you think meditation is for loonies, rest assured that aikido is quite different. Although it can be vigorous and is definitely effective for self-defense, all its movements are natural and nonviolent. We find aikido's emphasis on coordination carries over to many aspects of daily life – our physical condition is improving as our body awareness and powers of concentration advance very rapidly.

☯

Japan's Meiji Restoration of 1868 established a system of civil rights that, in many ways, remained more advanced than the U.S. system for over a century. No longer could samurai kill with impunity. The new martial art of Ueshiba allowed self-defense without necessarily causing death or even serious injury to the attacker.

The implications of this were mighty. Let's explore them in our next management challenge.

Management Challenge: *Steve is a police officer.* He was trained to draw his firearm only when absolutely necessary, but to shoot to kill an armed assailant. In ten years with the police force, he's also had ample experience in dirty street fighting. He believes "shoot to kill" is the right doctrine, but he wants to handle inebriated minors and mentally ill street people with less violent techniques than those he learned at the academy and on the street. He attends aikido classes when he is off duty.

Joanne owns a small retail business. She read that a burglar won a court judgment against a similar business for injuries sustained during a break-in. She wonders what the world is coming to. She wants to feel safe in her store and during her commute. She sees her neighbors carrying guns and hiding behind triple locks and house alarms. Joanne won't keep a gun in her apartment because she has a young child. Knowing that her armed neighbors don't attend regular gun safety and marksmanship classes actually makes Joanne feel *less* secure! And noting her neighbors are still fearful after spending all that money on guns and locks, she decides, "I don't want to live in fear. If safety is really important to me, I'm going to put in the time and effort to learn to protect myself." Her lawyer explains the principle of escalation of force, pointing out that gun-toters, knowing only one, lethal level of response to a threat, could find themselves in terrible legal trouble. Learning that aikido offers many response levels – avoid, evade, control, throw, disarm, injure – Joanne embarks on a twice-weekly study of the art.

Jack cares for troubled and mentally ill teens at a state hospital. It is usually a peaceful job, but every once in a while one of the young clients will get hold of a can opener and lunge at another teen, or at Jack. Jack understands the teens' psychological problems, and knows there's no real malice behind these nonetheless dangerous attacks. He doesn't want to hurt the kids more than they've been hurt already, and his boss wants no return visits from the reporter who wrote about a prior incident of a caregiver breaking a client's arm. Jack chances onto an aikido class and learns aikido techniques are just right for taking sharp objects away from angry clients, without injuring them or himself.

Terry was with the U.S. forces assigned to peacekeeping duty in Kosovo. He quickly learned there was no enemy to fight, and that U.S. forces were not supposed to act like invaders. Breaking up scuffles and rock throwing incidents among civilian factions was beyond his Army training, but a sergeant who had trained in aikido taught Terry some simple control and immobilization techniques that he then used almost daily while stationed in the Balkans.

Sheila is a flight attendant for a large airline. A beautiful woman who is slender of build, she has been training in aikido for ten years and holds a black belt, in addition to a number of first-aid certifications. Sheila is comfortable with most situations involving unruly or ill passengers, even knowing that the nearest ambulance is thirty thousand feet straight down. Her aikido training lets her read the intention and psycho-physiological state of her customers, and she solves many problems before they are even visible to other passengers and crew.

Aikido principles can help explain corporate culture. Often, culture manifests itself as a communal belief that some course of action is impossible. Many of the impressive mind-body effects practiced in aikido are quite simple but outside the experience of most people. It is easy in a classroom to get a student opinion leader to state that a given task can't be done. (If there's someone in the class built like a football lineman, I'll ask him to hunker down in a defensive posture. I then ask the opinion leader to move the athlete by pushing on his shoulder. Usually, the student can't do it.) Other students, if they can be persuaded to try, will also certainly fail to do it. To finish the demonstration, I show that it can be done easily. To persuade the students that there was no "cheating," I teach them to do it too. The students take the point that business opportunities are missed if we too easily accept the social consensus that an action is impossible.

Frank Doran Sensei describes blending in aikido this way: If your attacker says "North!," you don't say "South!" You say, "Yes, I see why you think north is so nice. Now have you ever tried south?" This is not just a metaphor for physical technique, but suggests a "verbal aikido" that is effective in negotiation and conflict management in the business world. It is not the usual style in academic argument, though, where it is more common to say bluntly,

"I don't agree," or "ridiculous!" Yes, getting to "life all of one piece" is hard, but these days I use verbal aikido almost exclusively, even in academe.

There is, however, still a place for bluntness. At the market research company where I worked, an executive of a major food manufacturer argued with my market numbers. I knew (and I think he knew I knew) that he had no grounds for criticizing my method, and that he was trying to make his department's sales look better at bonus time. It was within his power to terminate our account. In a large meeting, he tried repeatedly to tear my method apart, and finally asked loudly, "What if I still don't believe your numbers are any good?" I told him, essentially, that we could step outside and settle it there. Those in the room who were *conscious* enough to read between the lines understood I was not seriously suggesting violence as a way of settling the question. Standing my ground on what had become an ethical question, I was helping save face by not placing the ethical issue explicitly on the table. The numbers were accepted and the bill was paid.

Exercise: How reactive are you? You will need a friend to help you with this exercise, but do not attempt it unless you both are in a relaxed frame of mind, and you have some floor space far from anything that might be tripped over. Stand with your feet parallel and shoulder-width apart, your hands hanging at your sides. Your friend will stand at your right shoulder, facing ninety degrees to your left. To illustrate the effect of "thoughts buzzing around your head like flies," first imagine that a fly has actually landed on top of your head. The fly is drawing your attention to the top of your head, as you wonder what it is doing up there! Your friend will now place the flats of the fingers of his left hand in the hollow of your right shoulder, and push gently toward your back. Notice how this feels, and whether anything happens.

Now, the next stage of the exercise: Imagine the fly has landed again, at a spot on your lower abdomen about three or four finger-widths below your navel. To help you further concentrate on this spot (the *hara* in martial art jargon), tell yourself that you are hearing your friend's voice not through your ears but through your hara. When he again pushes on your shoulder, pretend you feel the pressure not on your shoulder, but in your hara. None of these things are true, but telling yourself a few little lies can help focus your attention at the hara. How does it feel now when your friend pushes against your shoulder?

Switch roles, and test your friend, with him imagining the fly landing first on his head, then on his lower abdomen. Express to each other how your experience differs according to where you have placed your attention, and whether you found the concentration easy or difficult.

Most people will have to step backward when the "fly" is on their head. The friend's light push will feel like a surprise, and cause a loss of balance. In contrast, when the concentration is on the hara, the friend can push much harder, usually with no overt effect. The person being tested is aware of the push, but finds it easily tolerable, nothing that has to be reacted to.

Of course this exercise doesn't suggest you can stop a speeding locomotive. Stay off those railroad tracks! What it does suggest is that your body's ability to withstand an assault changes according to your state of mind. What I'd like to focus on for this chapter's take-away tool is a different lesson from the exercise: When you think about your hara, you increase your ability to keep your autonomy of action. Remember that when you were thinking about the top of your head, you stepped back without meaning to, because of a very light touch from your partner. You were being hyper-reactive, responding to an inconsequential stimulus.

Being hyper-reactive is bad because it wastes effort that could be devoted to more important things (for example, your practice or your mission). It is bad because it lets other people control your actions! When you are "all in your head" and you are pushed, you will either step back or fall down. When you are pushed while conscious and centered, you may do nothing, or step back, push back, turn, or walk away. When centered at hara, you keep not only your autonomy but your full range of choices as to how and whether to respond. Moreover, you feel good afterward, not agitated and resentful as you most probably feel after you over-react to a minor annoyance.

Tool: *React only when you really have to.* Soon you will have a day at the office when your preoccupation with work problems will combine with incessant interruptions from your employees, to create a state of hyper-reaction. Your internal agitation, possibly building on your ego investment in being the boss, will drive you to "do something" about each issue brought to you by your co-workers. Do not! Take a deep breath and find your hara. The next time an employee pops in with a minor crisis, say, "Please take care of it as you think best," or "Why have you brought this to me?" Better yet, just smile pleasantly.

If you predictably and invariably reply, "I'll take care of it," you rob your employees of chances for initiative. Worse, you encourage them to take the low road in any situation – that is, to deal with it by manipulating the boss. And you will leave yourself feeling stressed and overburdened.

In martial art, being centered at hara brings a wide, clear awareness of one's surroundings, conducive to good self-defense. Its management analog is "seeing the big picture." When we see the big picture, we have a heightened, balanced awareness of what is important and urgent. Practice serving yourself and others by not reacting to the inconsequential.

Q Now you're confusing me. Zen is supposed to let us react spontaneously and instantaneously. If I'm thinking about the top of my head and step back when someone pushes me, I'm not premeditating that either, but you say that's bad. How can I tell the difference between instant reactions that are right and instant reactions that are wrong?

A This is no Zen paradox. Examine your feelings. If a push or other interruption leaves you shocked and upset, you were in a reverie-induced hyper-reactive state. If you feel calm, accepting, and instantly ready to deal with additional challenges, then you were unattached to your prior mental state; you were well-centered.

A brief earthquake struck suddenly when Tesshu Yamaoka, one of Japan's most prominent 19th-century Zen teachers, was leading a student over a mountain path. The student fell to the ground, and asked Yamaoka, "Sensei, why didn't you fall down?" He replied, "There was no time to fall down." He was telling his student that the earthquake had not been prolonged enough to cause a fall directly. The student, Tesshu implied, fell down as a reaction to his own fears.

True budo is a work of love. It is a work of giving life to all beings, and not killing or struggling with each other. Love is the guardian deity of everything. Nothing can exist without it. Aikido is the realization of love.
- Morihei Ueshiba

Courtesy in Martial Art and Business

Any instructor will tell you that martial arts begin and end with courtesy. Why is this?

One reason for rules of etiquette in aikido *classes* is that aikido *technique* (waza) has no rules. The techniques are based on fundamental principles. In action, the principles are expressed without pattern, premeditation, or rules. This requires great concentration. Behavior not directly related to waza, like how we enter the practice area, or ask the instructor for help, is standardized so that our fellow students are not distracted from what is really important in the training. In this way, courtesy has great practical value.

Also at the practical level, courteous behavior minimizes the chances of injured honor that can lead to enmity or vendetta.

A greater reason is that courtesy is the outward form of respect, and we hope to develop respect for our partners in practice. When we respect someone, we pay attention to his needs and wants, so that we can harmonize with him. Have you heard the phrase "to know her is to love her"? By paying attention and knowing our partner, we come to feel compassion, and, if we are lucky, the universal love that is at the heart of aikido. We can't see or enforce respect and love, but we can and do enforce courtesy in the dojo – and at the office.

Our commitment to courtesy is a reminder that we wish to conduct ourselves and our businesses at a level above simple coercion, blackmail and gang rule. And surely, paying attention to customers' wants and needs is the essence of marketing.

Physicians take an oath to do no harm. Lawyers swear to uphold the U.S. Constitution. Aikidoists who appear unable to uphold high standards are not given their black belts. But what about MBA students, who, these days, have an equal impact on our society? They graduate if they get adequate grades in their technical courses, and they're not required to swear to a single thing. This should change. Meanwhile, courtesy can be enforced in class, and a student's commitment to courtesy is a reminder of his or her responsibility to society.

Some of today's CEOs have legendary tempers. Apple employees call

Steve Jobs' blowups "Stevetrums." The press says Hewlett-Packard's Lew Platt didn't hesitate to loudly dramatize his irritation at bad performance. Considering what such CEOs are paid per minute, it is clear that stockholders don't get a positive return on investment during executive tantrums.

The news is full of school shootings, violent hate crimes, murderous day traders and postal workers, road rage, and even airplane passenger rage. In Medford, Oregon, a 27-year-old jobless man with an MBA blamed his college degree for his murder of three people. "There are too many business grads out there," he said. "If I had chosen another field, all this may not have happened." Each of these news items shows the result of cherishing anger until anger takes over, explodes, and harms more than one person.

Feeling anger is not a problem. Being possessed by anger is a problem. Do I ever feel anger? Of course I do; I'm human. Sometimes the anger lasts a short time, and sometimes it lasts a longer time. It is certain to last a long time if I clasp the anger to my bosom, if I am seduced to believe I am the anger and the anger is me, if I am attached to the anger and its adrenaline rush.

Back to basics then: The first step is to loose the attachment to the anger. The anger is the anger, and I am me. Two distinct entities. The connection between the two can be slack or tight. It's my choice.

Second step: Can I learn anything from the brief feeling of anger?

Management Challenge: "Probably," thought Pam, "I can think of a way this situation could have been avoided while still getting the project done on time and on budget and on quality. Am I really mad at my colleague Joe, or mad at the company for letting things get to this point, or mad at myself for not seeing it coming?" Pam is trying to separate herself from her frustration over a corporate snafu, and learn what can be learned. She continues her thought, "If I'm mad at myself, I'll know not to take it out on Joe, and I'll know what I need to learn to make sure this doesn't happen again. But I don't want to be needlessly hard on myself. If it's really Joe's fault, that has to be dealt with."

Third step: Is there any point at all to prolonging the anger? No. The answer is always no. It's harmful to her health. Pam knows there are lots of ways to change Joe's behavior other than exploding at him. If she is mad enough at the company and can't do anything about it, she will adopt a new mission, "Find a new job." It might then be constructive for Pam to briefly recall her anger, if she needs more motivation to spend her evenings answering want ads.

Tool: *Three rules for dealing with anger.*

1. Understand and loosen up your attachment to your anger.
2. Ask yourself what you can learn from the anger you feel.
3. Ask yourself whether the anger can be turned to constructive purpose. Can you put all that energy to good use?

After you have completed these three steps, you can leave your anger behind. With practice and meditation, you will find the three steps becoming quick and automatic. *Dallas Business Journal* editor Glenda Vossburgh uncovered what Sir Francis Bacon (1561-1626) had to say about anger: "There is no other way but to meditate." Vossburgh reports a 1996 survey finding that a quarter of U.S. employees are at least somewhat angry at work on a continuing basis. She mentions the cost of this, not just in lives, but in multi-million dollar court awards, personnel turnover, workers' compensation claims, and reduced productivity. She suggests training managers to see trouble brewing before it bubbles over, providing employees a safe channel for reporting their frustrations, and training everyone in how to defuse confrontations.

Talking to an employee about her temper has legal implications for the employer. Zen martial art expertise can augment a firm's legal expertise by helping managers help the angry person see her ego involvement in the situation. This can defuse the anger or even turn anger into laughter. It helps managers keep their own egos out of the interaction; when one has nothing to prove and nothing to defend, one cannot be provoked.

As long as employee empowerment is given only lip service, employee frustration will build. The conscious manager is committed to continuing education, spares no effort to match the right people with the right jobs, and lets employees put their best foot forward. All these reduce frustration and offer employees the chance of fulfillment.

Outside the walls of the organization, companies can forestall customer rage by treating customers decently. Schools can require courses in the sophisticated and powerful methods of conflict resolution. Anthropologists are beginning to understand how the rank and file can cooperate to undermine harmful power structures in an organization. This can be taught. The knowledge can be boiled down to sitcom plots and billboard slogans. Slogans and sitcoms got us to stop smoking; perhaps they could get us to stop hugging our anger.

People are angry when they fear their own powerlessness. Unfortunately there are those who profit from these feelings and try to exacerbate them. TV anchors tease, "Your car may be unsafe – story at eleven." Each political party wants us to be mad at the others. Selling fear is so much easier than marketing beneficial products. I picture MBA dropouts doing the P.R. for hate groups, evening news shows, and politicians.

A martial art analogy: Suppose Mr. Mugger swings a stick at my head. He would like me to think the stick is my immediate problem. While I am distracted by the stick, he's getting ready to kick me. As an experienced aikidoist, I know my real problem is Mr. Mugger, not his stick. I move toward him directly, to execute a defense. Similarly, our cars are not our enemies; fear-mongering TV anchors and producers are. Once that's clear, we can take steps as citizens and customers to counter the spells of fear that they weave.

Tool: *Courtesy opens the door of awareness and distances us from anger.* Start to give special attention to "please" and "thank you" with each and every person you encounter – especially with people you have been taking for granted. Notice changes in your organization's atmosphere, productivity and sales. Next, recognize when someone is selling fear. Your courtesy, even to a person like this, serves as a buffer between his pitch and your fast gut reaction to it. It will give you time to distance yourself from any anger you feel toward him or toward yourself. It will send him a message that at least one person won't buy what he's selling!

A last, happily vulgar, note on the futility of cherishing anger: Why did the mouse have to run up the elephant's leg three times? Because the first two times, he got pissed off.

I am calm however and whenever I am attacked. I have no attachment to life or death. I leave everything as it is to God. Be apart from attachment to life and death and have a mind which leaves everything to Him, not only when you are being attacked but also in your daily life.
- Morihei Ueshiba

It is not our darkness we fear most. It is our greatness, our light.
- Nelson Mandela

Working for Change – and I Don't Mean Nickels

It's hard to get people to change. That's the conclusion of anyone who has ever tried to innovate in an organization.

This page starts with Ueshiba O-Sensei's words about attachment to life and death. What do change and death have to do with each other? Let's entertain the idea that fear of change is a disguised fear of death. By examining the merits of this startling idea, we will find new courage in dealing with change and new perspectives on managing change.

My management consultant friends don't even mention this idea at their seminars. "People don't want to hear that," says one. "If I talk about death, they want their money back." Indeed, I attended a seminar given by one friend where this topic was tackled head on – and the seminar was never repeated. If the subject makes you uncomfortable, you may take it slowly, or skip the chapter for now. But the subject is an indispensable part of your Zen training, and if you are serious about becoming a conscious manager, you must come back to it before long.

Can a healthy person overcome the drive of the cells, the DNA, to live, and develop a perfect indifference to death? Rarely. Can a balanced person reduce the fear of death to a bare minimum? Definitely. And this is much more powerful than perfect indifference. The statement of a Christ on the cross or a monk immolating himself on the streets of Saigon would make us feel only pity if we thought he was crazy or without care. Kazantzakis' *The Last Temptation of Christ* shows us it is the martyr's lingering fear and doubt that make his death a true sacrifice. They tell us, "Here is a sane person who has chosen to fight this fight, no matter the cost." A compassionate bodhisattva, an enlightened person who has taken on the mission of helping others toward enlightenment, must, by definition, feel at least an echo of what we ordinary folks feel.

It is possible to develop this "bare minimum" without sacrificing one's life, but instead, to live life with a commitment to a chosen mission. A conscious manager committed to a mission is then uncluttered by anxieties about his own mortality, and is a much more effective manager of his mission.

How can fear of death be reduced to a minimum? Let's answer this in an indirect way, with an exercise illustrating the futility of holding too tightly to ego.

Exercise: Think about the person you were when you were twelve years old. That person didn't want to die, but where is he today? Though he has some sort of continuity with your present personality, he no longer dominates your viewpoint, and is, in a manner of speaking, dead. But if you are lucky, he pops up from time to time – doesn't he? – to help you see things through youthful eyes and renew your perspective. When was the last time you "saw" your inner twelve-year-old? Was it a pleasant encounter? Are you glad you are no longer twelve and no longer act like a twelve year old?

It is true that our growth beyond age twelve is not the same as the final death of our body. But the point of the exercise is that each of our ego manifestations, at every age, passes away. Looking back, we are not always sorry about its passing. This is true not just of the ego, but of the body itself; scientists say every molecule of a human body cycles out in the course of nine years. (Thus, I can tease my wife of twenty-three years with the notion that she is really my third wife.) All living things grow and change, or at least should grow and change. It seems incredible that people can mistake growth and change for oblivion, but sadly it happens every day.

Management Challenge: Bob's retirement. You have worked, as I have, with people like Bob. Bob is affable, intelligent and, on occasion, even wise. But life has hit Bob with a one-two punch that makes him poisonous to himself and to the firm. He has never developed interests outside the office, and he has not come to grips with his mortality.

As a result, Bob is hanging on long after he should let go. He identifies himself with his job. As retirement looms, he panics because he understands he doesn't know who he is. His business decisions, previously often brilliant, are now entwined with ego maintenance, and they suffer in quality. He snipes at co-workers and subordinates, and increasingly says "I..." when he used to say "This company..."

Bob is showing attachment to his mission and to a false sense of his identity. The person closest to Bob should point out to him that the crisp manner he used to make decisions in the past might best be used now to map his own future. Throughout his career, Bob focused his management attention where it was most needed, and now is the time for a new needs assessment. Bob's fixed idea that the company is the only worthwhile object of his management skills is, like all fixed ideas, one that should be re-examined. Bob may relish the idea, once it is pointed out to him, that directing his considerable talents at objectives and strategies for retirement might produce great results.

Healthy people respect their own lives and do not want to die, nor do they fear death. Zen philosophy tells us it is not the experience of fear, but the clinging to fear, that clogs up our free-flowing enlightenment. Fear of death is different from fear of other events. If a manager is afraid, for example, of making a public speech, she will enjoy the lifting of the fear the day after the speech, even if she has not conquered the fear prior to the speech. And she will be able to learn from the experience. These things are not true about death. If this manager does not conquer her fear of death before the event, she will suffer from it her whole life long.

There are five demons that feed our fear of death. Luckily, there exist swords with which the conscious manager may conquer these demons.

Demon #1: If I were dead, I might miss something interesting. Bless you for being interested in life, but there is some egoism in this. The world does not exist for your entertainment. Have you contributed to the entertainment (or the greater wealth, health and succor) of others? That is all you can ask from life. If you are addicted to the excitement of current events and fear their lack, then you have an attachment problem. As we learned earlier, attachment can be cured; meditation is one sword that can cut attachment. On your better days, you have realized that every ordinary thing is a miracle. So are you making too much distinction between what is "interesting" and what is not?

Demon #2: I feel so good today, I want it to go on forever. You need a similar sword to cut the attachment to feeling good. What luck you have had, compared to the many who have suffered more or less since birth. Have you helped any of them? Once you have done so, you will feel a satisfaction that, while it may invite an addiction of its own, is more lasting than the passing endorphin rush. The universe's patterns are imprinted on you, and your patterns imprinted on it. So, willing or not, you are connected to everyone and everything. Your feelings of contentedness, of power, and of immortality should all flow from that fact.

Demon #3: No one else can do my job as well as I can; I'd better stick around. Have you trained an apprentice to take over in the event of your disability? If you have not, then you have shirked your responsibility, and youare *not* the best person for your job. Naturally you are more experienced than your apprentice, and she is not yet as skilled as you, but giving her a chance to succeed or fail independently is also part of your responsibility.

Demon #4 (the Return On Investment demon): Society (and my family) invested a lot in my education; I need to protect their investment. We hope they did not educate you to be fearful. Given that they did not, what did they educate you *for?* It was so you could find a worthwhile mission and pursue it effectively, that is, without distracting fears. (Does "effectively" mean you must make excessive – and ultimately fruitless – investments to ensure your own survival during your mission? No, that would be Demon #3 talking. See above.)

Demon #5: I must be here to see that my children are protected and provided for. This is the toughest demon of all. Don't put off spending the time with your children that is required to raise them properly and teach them love and responsibility. Do it now. Schedule it in your day-timer if that's what it takes. Buy life insurance. Draw up a will.

All living things must grow and change. Human living things have a unique plasticity, an extreme ability to adapt our knowledge, attitudes, body, brain, and capabilities. We prove it by occupying more ecological niches – caves to condos, cattle ranches to corporate cubicles, and Sahara to South Pole – than any other higher organism. To be human is to choose to be better or worse, and then to go ahead and change for the better or change for the worse. To succumb to the fear of change is to refuse to transform oneself toward greater godliness – when it is perfectly clear that people *can* make this transformation. To reject one's own potential is such a gigantic sin that I wonder why there is no common name for it.

Yes, a sin, and we all know lots of people who are guilty, guilty, guilty. We sympathize with their fears that they may not be able to do a different job, use different equipment, or change their ways. We may worry about their karma.

We wonder about their childhood influences. Who could have molded such fearful people, and why? To be fearful is pitiable, but to make other people fearful is an outrage, an evil.

Many consultants speak of the fear of change, but few speak of the numbing grind of unchanging, repetitive jobs. A manager who ensures that employees fear change more than they fear changelessness is evil indeed.

Q I work with people who fear change, and also with people who encourage their employees to fear change. What can I do?

A First, work on yourself. Study and follow the path of the conscious manager. Next, be a good example. Watching you, your colleagues and employees will see that there better ways to deal with change. Do not confront destructive managers in an argumentative way; that will merely feed their fears and insecurities. Do feel free to quietly suggest words and alternatives to them at key moments.

All living things must grow and change. And here is an irony: If a manager cleaves to his current identity and resists all change, he is nailing shut the coffin of that twelve-year old inside him. His earlier self can no longer delight him by popping in every now and then. He is making sure that twelve-year-old's fears of oblivion come true. He is the molded and the molder. Here is a person who, to use a Zen-ish phrase now in fashion, needs to get over himself.

Downsized executives go to outplacement consultants, who counsel them on the stages of grief, as if downsizing were a death sentence. That premise is wrong. A chance to change is a chance to live.

I ran an experiment in an MBA class, asking, "Is fear of change fear of death, in disguise?" The very idea made most of the class uncomfortable. Nervous laughs rippled across the room. One student asked, "Are you saying that people who fear change more, fear death more?" This wasn't a totally accurate restatement of my query. But the student's question did crystallize the ideas of this chapter, and made it clear that our straw man argument was incorrect: People do not fear change because they fear death. *People fear change because they fear life.*

Dogen Zenji and Ueshiba O-Sensei both remarked, obscurely, that each day they spent time on both sides of the mortal veil. As we ponder the surprising difficulty of distinguishing between fear of death and fear of life, we can gain, if not full understanding, at least a glimmer of what the two masters meant.

☯

Zen philosophy does not include ideas of good and evil. This fact shocks Westerners who are interested in Zen but bring to it, due to their religious upbringing, an admirable impulse to be good people. In the introduction to this book, I said Zen can, nonetheless, lead to moral behavior in the sense such people would understand it. How can this be?

In *The Way of Zen*, Alan Watts explained it beautifully. Grasping is the outward manifestation of attachment. Zen, says Watts, teaches us that grasping at wealth, certainty, or advantage is fruitless, and most of what we in the West regard as immoral – theft, slavery, murder, etc. – is the result of grasping behavior. (Business people will appreciate that they are not advised against having wealth or acquiring it – just against compulsively clutching at it.)

The Zen practitioner lives in the present, but also accepts *karma*. Karma simply means cause and effect. In the West we consider the disregard of consequences as the very definition of evil. The awareness, arising from zazen, of the connectedness of things makes the practitioner sensitive to causes and effects and loath to disregard them. Compassion, then, is not a moral imperative, but a simple reality stemming from our interconnectedness, an issue of mental health rather than morality.

Nor does Zen involve believing in (in the Dalai Lama's slightly awkward phrase) "external beings," including deities. All Zen allusions to demons should be understood as metaphorical references to conflicting forces within ourselves.

In the first part of this chapter, I use the words "sin" and "evil." It should now be clear they are there simply for rhetorical impact.

In the chapter's opening quotation, Ueshiba O-Sensei defers to God. It is not clear to what extent O-Sensei's Omoto-kyo, a Shinto sect, literally believed in external deities; when asked, O-Sensei allegedly replied, "That's my religion. Go get your own." In any case, though O-Sensei was not speaking in a Zen context, conscious managers will be well guided by his wisdom about life and death.

Opening

Man cannot approach the divine by reaching beyond the human; he can approach them by becoming human. To become human is what he, this individual man, has been created for.... Men do not find God if they stay in this world. They do not find Him if they leave the world.
- Martin Buber, *I and Thou*

In an extraordinary moment, the entire world seems condensed in the fall of a leaf from a branch.

At a political rally, one's heart opens with empathy for everyone who is scratching to make a living. It is a vivid realization that we're all in this together.

While climbing a rock face, the intense concentration and loss of the sense of self cause the climber to feel at one with the breeze, the sunshine, the cliff, and its history.

A thoughtful manager is struck by his utter dependence on the air and food the earth provides, on the people who bring it to him, and on the sun that powers the whole process. He begins to question his self-image as an autonomous individual.

The experience of awe at the birth of a child.

A close brush with death causes an epiphany about the preciousness of life, the necessity of death, and the beauty of life's renewal.

Each of these is an opening experience, an essential step on the path of conscious management. It may change the manager's views and actions for a day or for a lifetime.

Don't expect to practice hard and not experience the weird. Hard practice that evades the unknown makes for a weak commitment.
- Kyong Ho (1849-1912)

And Yet   *there are so many islands,*
sep-
                     arated
              in the brain.
       Walk across the channels.   *Follow*
                    a sandpiper.
           Will any of us be there?
- Patricia Goedicke

On the Extraordinary

One day when I was still in the *kyu* (pre-black belt) ranks, the class was doing a forward rolling drill. We had formed two lines at opposite corners of the practice mat. The first person in each line would run full speed to the mat's center. Just as collision was imminent, the runner from one line would suddenly kneel on all fours, and the other would do a forward fall over his kneeling partner. There were beginners in the class who performed this movement very awkwardly, so the exercise continued for at least twenty minutes. More experienced students started doing crazy variations in order to stay interested.

On my next turn, I found myself facing Mark. Mark and I had gone to high school together, and we had just returned from some months of training together at Ki Society headquarters in Tokyo. He was my closest friend, and we were sensitized to each other's movements on the mat. For these reasons, and out of semi-boredom with the exercise, I ran to the center of the mat with total abandon and without premeditating the forward roll in any way. I remember seeing Mark's nose a few inches from my own and closing fast.

The next thing I knew I was somewhere near the gym's 15-foot ceiling, looking downward, with events proceeding in slow motion. I saw Mark on all fours on the mat, and the other class members staring upward with their mouths open. I had never jumped this high before in my life. In fact, people are not supposed to be able to jump this high, Olympic athletes possibly excepted. In this pause, my self-consciousness returned. I remember thinking, "Hey, how am I going to get down from here?"

I hit the mat awkwardly but safely. As I stood, everyone in the class – except Mark, of course, who didn't see any of this – was wide-eyed, saying "Wow!" and "How did you do that?". Even Armando, who was teaching that day, and who was normally extremely cool and fazed by nothing, allowed himself a smile and a "Way to go, Fred!". But the irony was that I didn't feel it was "Fred" who "did" that extraordinary feat. Certainly, if I tried to do it again, I couldn't.

Aikido students become accustomed to seeing unusual things and small miracles during every class. For instance, during weapons practice, when many people swing big sticks in all directions in a small room, it is rare for anyone to get hit. A group consciousness and coordination seems to develop. For this reason, the class regarded my levitation stunt simply as a pleasing validation of our joint practice. More surprising than most, but nothing to call in to *Sports Illustrated*.

Many years later, the time came for my third *dan* (3rd degree black belt) examination in Chicago. Toyoda Sensei called for *hanmi hantachi randori*, a multiple-person attack with me kneeling and allowed to walk only on my knees while my attackers locomoted normally. I made a mistake – I did something that Sensei had not five minutes before told a 2nd degree candidate not to do – and I was mentally kicking myself for it, when one of my attackers actually did kick me. I remember Gary's knee connecting with my temple, and then I blacked out. I'm talking total amnesia, but somehow I must have kept moving.

When I came to, we were bowing to each other and everyone was applauding. I wondered whether the applause was for me and what I had done. When the test was over, Toyoda Sensei kept saying, "Good test, good test."

I'll never know what I was doing while I was unconscious. But my aikido friends' applause led me to believe that whatever my body did while I was "missing" was true aikido; that I did not appear disoriented, or passive, or (my worst fear) violent. This was a great relief and satisfaction.

As a footnote to this story, during the test's final multiple attack – a standing *randori* – I let myself get distracted by my attackers' hands. My energy was rising to my upper body, and I was losing mobility. Disaster was near, but just then Gary landed another kick, right on my butt. It was like being struck by the wooden *kyosaku* slat while sitting zazen. It startled me into another reality where everything was crystal clear and in slow motion. I kept moving and ended the randori, and the test, with energy to spare.

The following year, the Aikikai group in Austin had a visit from Robert Nadeau. Nadeau Sensei is well known as one of the first westerners to have studied under aikido's founder, and I was curious to meet him. During his public seminar at the University of Texas, I was his *uke*, providing the needed mock attacks as he demonstrated the hip throw *koshi nage*. While he lectured and answered students' questions, my feet left the ground many times. To save

50

time, Sensei did not complete the throw at any time while he spoke, but he repeatedly demonstrated positioning and efficient lifting. When he asked the class to take partners and try the technique, I relaxed, expecting him to again place me on the mat.

Wrong! He levered me over his hip and high into the air. My body was perfectly vertical, and I saw the ground approaching my nose at what seemed like sixty miles per hour. I remember my thought: "If I try to plan this landing, I'm going to die." Maybe that was an exaggeration, and maybe not, but my next thought was the crux of this story: "There's a part of me that knows how to do this." Again my conscious mind blanked out, and when I woke up I had just completed a break-fall, in which slapping the mat with the arm reduces the rest of the body's impact against the mat. I could judge this from the tingling in my forearm. I was unhurt, and the class was looking at us and making "ooh" and "aah" noises. "Fred," the head of the University of Texas dojo said, "I didn't know you could break-fall that well."

The same dubious mechanism won my reputation in Portland aikido. In 1996, I attended the seminar of a visiting shihan, who took a moment to correct my technique. Because he is a famous man, scores of people watched him give me instruction, and continued to watch as a strong shodan, the kind of fellow we seniors call "young meat," attacked me with full force. The technique required a complex movement on my part, quickly done and perfectly timed. Again I blanked, coming to a moment later, to see the young man on the floor. One student sitting nearby whistled, "Ooh, that was pretty."

Many teachers have warned us not to be enchanted, or even distracted, by supra-normal phenomena. They happen, but they are not the focus of our practice. They happen, but they should not be pursued. When they happen, they are just, in Ram Dass' phrase, "grist for the mill." Fascination with magic can lead to a disconnection from one's practice and one's fellows – or worse, as the Sorcerer's Apprentice learned. Stick to your practice and discipline. The magic may just be there when you need it most.

In all of these stories, my "self," or the conscious part of my brain, was temporarily absent or shut down. Were these instances of the mu-shin our teachers speak of, the no-mind that we read about? It would be a shame if when you transcend your self, your self can't be around to appreciate it, or even remember it.

A friend who is a Zen sensei implied my blackout phenomenon, far from being a good Zen no-mind, might be a neural defect. She saw I was intrigued by its mysterious nature. I think she was suggesting I ought to get un-intrigued. Her constructive suggestion, slightly tinged with personal insult, was a loving attack against my ego, and very Zen. It didn't explain my olympic high-jump, though!

An oft-told Zen tale has one acolyte bragging about his master's ability to part the seas and do other assorted miracles. His fellow novice topped him by saying *his* master ate when he was hungry and slept when he was tired. This reminder of the value of quotidian practice is echoed for Westerners in what the business writer Adam Smith calls the "Ballad of the Zen Cowboy":

> I eat when I'm hungry,
> I drink when I'm dry.
> And if I'm lucky,
> I'll live 'till I die.

I enjoy speculating about consciousness and about the meaning of these stories. Although the brain can reorganize itself to "back up" or replicate the functions of damaged areas (and in this sense the mind is unified), at any given time different areas of the brain control different functions. Experiments have shown that severing the connections between "departments" can produce bizarre results. A person with a certain sort of brain lesion, for example, can look at a picture of a lifelong friend, and say, "Yes, I know that person," but be unable to say the friend's name. So recognition and naming reside in two separate departments.

The experiences I've related to you suggest a number of things about brain organization. My memory of aikido technique seems to be accessible even when my self-consciousness department is shut down. I can't recall or verbalize experiences that occurred at such times. It could be that verbalization is necessary for conscious memory, or that the self-consciousness department is somehow necessary for converting short-term memories into long-term memories. Sense and muscle abilities seem to work okay without the help of the self-consciousness department, meaning that sensory and motor signals don't always travel through the self-consciousness department. Finally, my "there's a part of me that knows how to do this" experience with Nadeau Sensei suggests the brain's departments can behave with remarkable autonomy, almost like separate persons renting space inside one's head. It shows one can learn to voluntarily shut down the self-consciousness department when the situation calls for it, and shunt control over to that "someone else" who resides somewhere inside us.

It's confusing to think about "departments" and "connections" when Zen martial art teaches that the mind and body are a unity. How can it be that we can function better when one of our brain's departments is disconnected – that is, when our minds are fragmented? It's a paradox that arises often in our practice. Like all paradoxes, this one is a challenge for scientific inquiry, a lesson on the limitations of language, and a *koan* (a riddle-lesson) for the Zen practitioner.

How can we train ourselves to perform spontaneously and without conscious direction? Obviously, every technique must be practiced thousands of times so that we learn it deeply, throughout our bodies. We will then "perform

52

with confidence," as Koichi Tohei Sensei has put it, and be willing to let go ofconscious control.

Besides training hard, we must try at times to put ourselves in high-pressure situations in the training hall or the board room that may lead to self-transcendence. This includes (in aikido) taking advancement tests at every opportunity. During a test, our fellow students applaud and cheer for us. This is to give us energy and reinforce our behavior, not to feed our egos. We are also nervous and anxious to put our best foot forward for our teachers and fellows. A test is an ordeal, but it is also an opportunity. This is what Toyoda Sensei means when he says, "A test is a gift."

Q I have an aversion to rank. My motivation is to improve myself. Nothing more. I have no need or desire to prove anything to others by achieving rank. Do you think it is bad for my training to shun testing? In other words, would going for promotions in rank in aikido improve my practice in any manner?

A Yes, it would. A test is a learning experience that is different from an ordinary aikido class, especially because in aikido we do not have tournaments. If you shun tests, it's just one class after another after another...

In addition, as you rise in rank, newer students turn to you for help, knowing you've "been through it." Helping them gives you a new perspective on your own practice, and so it helps you learn too. Being *sempai* (mentor) to newer students is also "dojo duty." In a dojo you must do more than pay monthly dues; I insist on dojo duty that involves helping each other learn.

The old adage "Never try to prove yourself, just try to improve yourself" has much merit. You should not regard tests primarily as a means of proving yourself to others. A test is simply a different kind of opportunity to improve yourself, and as such, is of great value.

All people, know this!
When you strike
a flowing river
no trace remains
in the water.
- Saigo Tanomo

The Dignity Debate

Zen rightly emphasizes the facing of one's own death. Every moment spent in denial is a moment stolen from our perception of the world as it is, a moment robbed from one's ability to exclaim with the poet, "Ah! The sound of the falling snow!"

The Zen emphasis on direct experience of the world is a warning about the ways words can mislead. Recent controversies about "assisted suicide" provide ample opportunities for denial and for ambiguous catch-phrases like "right to die" and "death with dignity." They make a perfect study in the conscious management of public policy, in the ways we decide how to vote on ballot measures dealing with this issue, and in the decisions made by corporations that affect health and death.

George Orwell's *1984* taught us that while individual acts of cruelty are limited in their impact, debasing our language opens the door to multitudes of evils. "Doctor-assisted suicide" is a perfect example. We are in deep trouble when we've forgotten that killing oneself is suicide; killing someone else is homicide.

Drawing our *wakizashi* (short sword), we cut the question into three more pieces:

1. The question of taking one's own life.
2. The question of granting responsibility for the ending of one's life to a family member, a friend, or a doctor, either explicitly or implicitly.
3. The question of making the accomplice's actions a matter of public record.

Society condemns the taking of one's own life. We encourage people who suffer from psychological or economic stress to seek help, instead of just ending it by suicide. While we may feel that there should be moral exceptions for sane people who are in final medical extremity, this distinction is difficult to write into law. The complicity of others in the ending of one's life is a matter of long tradition, and is not terribly controversial. In fact, it is even more common these days, as improved life-support technology requires more terminal patients' family members, after long and intense talks with the attending physician, to decide whether to "pull the plug" on the machines sustaining the unconscious patient.

Some compassionate physicians administer overdoses of narcotics to hopeless patients, and do so without the consent of the patient or the patient's family. Some desperate patients jump off bridges. In either case, individual responsibility is clear. In cases of consensual euthanasia, the motivations of both parties – and their ethical responsibility – will always remain in doubt. It is not your "right" to jump off a bridge, because it is illegal and it entails public expense and the chance of injuring others. Yet it is your right in the sense that no one can stop you from doing it, and it is possibly a superior moral choice because no physician becomes embroiled in questions of your motivations.

In the past, close social bonds among the patient's family, the physician, and the local community provided most of the needed checks and balances, and the courts generally did not become involved in the end-of-life decision. This was true whether the patient was unconscious or a conscious participant in the decision. (Conscious in the common sense of the word, not necessarily in our sense of "enlightened.") The surviving parties faced legal proceedings *if their action became known,* but the social ties also gave the participants a common reason to keep their action quiet and unofficial. Now, in communities where these social bonds may have weakened, it is the third question, public record, that is really at the heart of the heated debate.

Public disclosure of euthanasia (complicity in the ending of a terminal patient's life) is required when a government decides that such action is, under certain circumstances, legal. Where social bonds remain strong and public disclosure is required, communities fear that the reputation of their doctor (who is a trusted friend) and their neighbors may be destroyed if the courts decide the termination decision was borderline or improper. Where social bonds are weaker and euthanasia is legal, friends and family – and everyone who may become such a patient in the future – fear that the doctor will make a decision for reasons of cost or convenience. Legal permission, they may fear, reduces the doctor's moral responsibility. Students of history are familiar with the extreme end of state-sanctioned euthanasia, namely, the Nazis' mass extermination of ethnic populations deemed "socially diseased." In either case, then, making it legal may well make things worse.

Proponents of Oregon's "Death With Dignity Act" talk about the "solace of a quiet death." Most people today are not on speaking terms with death. A patient's fear of living may become more terrible than his fear of dying. But fear is not the right basis for decision, and if I were an M.D., I would not be able to take action on that basis.

If I were to kill in the heat of battle, while defending myself or others (against, say, a madman who is shooting up a restaurant and who clearly desires his own death more than the deaths of his innocent victims), I would be in severe legal jeopardy while witnesses sorted out what they saw and who shot first. Our traditions have always held that "cold-blooded" killing, that is, killing without violent provocation, should lead to even greater jeopardy. Yet that is exactly what, according to euthanasia legalization proponents, should carry no jeopardy for the physician. Where the act is illegal but socially tolerated, the shared sense of jeopardy binds the family and the community closer, which is what should happen after a death. No one can take the easy way out, hiding behind the letter of the law. The euthanasia decision will weigh heavily on all complicit parties. Their arguments and heartaches are a unifying experience.

People want to live and die within their own tradition and cultural matrix. Even Golden Gate jumpers leap from the city side of the bridge, making one last gesture toward social inclusion. One of James Michener's most riveting passages describes a nomadic tribe that crosses the violent Oxus River (between Afghanistan and China) twice yearly – by swimming. The old and sick do not make it to the other bank. Inhabitants of this harsh, spare land understand both the cruelty and the necessity of this practice. Cost considerations are a part of any cultural tradition.

Americans' fears that euthanasia decisions will be made primarily on the basis of cost (rather than compassion) are not overblown, however, and stem from our understanding that cultural values are not shared among all the actors. Nearly three quarters of workers with health insurance are cared for by corporations, the so-called "managed care providers." Health maintenance organizations (HMOs), with their huge medical resources and fixed monthly membership dues, raise patients' expectations about the care they will receive, and then sometimes (in cases that might be broadly publicized) dash these expectations, forcing the patient to sue the HMO in court. This is hardly conscious marketing. Moreover, when a long-term patient's cost of care exceeds his monthly membership dues, the HMO's economic interest and its legal obligation can be in conflict. Terminal patients in managed care might, under a law like Oregon's, be cared for by a physician who does not know the patient well and who is facing cost-containment pressures from corporate management. In Holland, where euthanasia is legal, surviving relatives suspect that these kinds of pressures have led to improper termination decisions in a number of cases.

Polls and press stories confirm that Americans don't believe corporations are preserving American traditions, or our various ethnic traditions; in fact we believe that corporations are dollarizing all of our cherished values. There have always been doctors who take on the immense personal responsibility, and the shattering psychological aftermath, of administering just a bit too much morphine. There have always been families that have shameful secrets, like the furtive unplugging of Uncle Max. Both are infinitely less scary than legally letting corporations persuade us, when we are weakest, to sign our own death warrants.

Management Challenge: *James Michener.* Ironically, decades after writing the passage mentioned above, and after losing his wife Mari and suffering from extreme and incurable diabetes, James Michener pulled his own plug. Living in Austin, Michener had spent his final days painfully hooked to a dialysis machine. The beloved writer settled his affairs, told his friends and doctors what he planned to do, and did it, taking sole responsibility.

I sympathize with all patients who are in pain and who feel they have lost control of their destiny. But I strongly suspect the traditional "no extraordinary measures" option is the best balance of individual rights and public safety. Our social and legal systems are not ready to support euthanasia, especially if we are so confused about its true meaning that we call it "doctor-assisted suicide."

In 2001, the Philip Morris Corporation reported to the Czech government that the early deaths of smokers reduce the amount paid out on smokers' state pensions. This reduction in social welfare costs, Philip Morris argued, benefited the Czech Republic's economy. Like other tobacco companies, Philip Morris is eager to forestall further government lawsuits and restrictions stemming from the social costs of cancers and lung disease due to smoking. But in this case, public outrage over the company's self-serving research was widespread and worldwide. This caper was as far from conscious management as a company can get. It was ghoulish, foolish and inhuman.

Corporations do what we as stockholders urge, allow, and abet. Again, we indulge in standing one step removed from responsibility. The result may be an instance where fear is, indeed, rational. When words can mean anything powerful corporations want them to mean, then no fears are excessive – if they lead to right action.

Conscious managers know most decisions have personal, organizational, social, legal and political dimensions. Zen principles lead conscious managers to emphasize the personal dimension, because it has to do with individual enlightenment, but never to ignore the other dimensions. This chapter's dissection of the euthanasia controversy suggests a number of conclusions:

- Just as each breath, each meal, and each step is a part of personal enlightenment, so is one's death. Ritual and tradition make death a focus of family and community life also. Any legal/political change that dilutes or devalues the personal and social dimensions of death must be approached with great caution. Informal control of illegal euthanasia can let bad decisions, and even some murders, go undetected. There is no evidence, though, that state-approved euthanasia would reduce wrongful deaths, and there are good arguments that it might increase them.

- Responsibility is part of enlightenment. While family and community involvement in end-of-life decisions is traditional and accepted, the person who wishes to manage his own life consciously will deal consciously with matters of responsibility for the life and death of himself and others.

- Rather than focus on individual and state responsibility for euthanasia, legal and political measures might better focus on the actions of corporations and other organizations whose actions affect our health. Recent government lawsuits against the tobacco companies show that action can be taken in that direction. National health insurance and regulation of HMOs are subjects needing more public discussion and possible action.

⬤ *Tool: Responsibility.* Responsibility is an important part of integrity. But it is a slippery concept, and subject to cultural relativity. In the U.S., we claim to admire individual responsibility, but we also have an exaggerated sense of individuality that limits our enlightenment. In Japanese industry, product development teams exist specifically to diffuse responsibility for success and failure. In Japanese stories involving huge, embarrassing failures, moreover, it is common for a servant or junior team member to accept the scapegoat role, even when he does not bear individual responsibility.

So this chapter gives you no further instructions about how to use the tool of responsibility. This is *your* opening. It is your opportunity to decide how to use responsibility, and how to make and use agreements with other people about the sharing of responsibility. Then you will be able to take a position on issues like end-of-life care that have corporate, public and family dimensions, and on the more everyday issues that arise in your managerial work.

Support

The young child has no direct knowledge of death, but has many experiences of paradox, which has the same structure as death. For example, the child may feel omnipotent since by the simple act of yelling, nurturance comes at his command. Then comes the dawning realization that his 'power' is a tribute paid to impotence. The baby's very life hangs upon the thread of parental solicitude.... This paradox of infancy yields to the larger paradox of adult existence itself.
- Charles Hampden-Turner, *Maps of the Mind*

Embarking on the path of consciousness, the manager is wise to "try with a little help from her friends." She is then on the stage of the path called "support."

Support may come in the form of a community with which to practice. It may be people with whom the manager can regroup and recoup after rigorous, exhausting practice. These people, even if they are not traveling the same path, converse with the conscious manager, listening and offering neither ridicule nor smothering sympathy.

The manager does not just take support, but consolidates her own learning by extending a helping hand to other members of the group.

61

In their efforts to pass beyond the intellect, the Zen Buddhists have emphasized the experience of the moment. Deliberation should not be permitted to interfere with the immediacy of the response. Just as the sound does not wait to issue forth when the bell is struck, man should develop that consciousness of mind that focuses infinite experience into instant intuition. The spontaneity of reaction is stressed continuously by the Zen master to his disciples. In the art of fencing the counter movements must be made without slow logic or hesitant reasoning. The intuition springs forth as a wordless and thoughtless message translated into integrated and immediate action.
- R.G.H. Siu

Zen and Creativity: Resources for Managers

In his book *Created in Japan,* Sheridan Tatsuno ventures that Zen precepts and practice can lead business people to greater creativity. Creativity is a necessary precursor to continued industrial innovation, and so is seen in Japan as critical to economic competitiveness. Zen principles promote creativity by giving practitioners insight into and control over the social and psychological habits that can prevent a direct, spontaneous and creative response to a situation or problem.

The number of Japanese who pursue esoteric Zen is tiny. Japanese companies do send employees to Zen temples for meditation retreats, but this, according to Professor Kunio Goto of St. Andrew's University, is for "psychotherapy," not for the pursuit of enlightenment. The free expression of creativity can be seen as eccentricity, especially in Japan. It is tolerated when displayed by Zen priests, but it is not tolerated among the general population, where group harmony is the paramount value.

Although enlightenment is said to be a monistic state, where individuality is revealed as illusion (Q: What did the Zen priest say to the hot dog vendor? A: "Make me one with everything."), the *paths* to enlightenment are known to be highly varied, individual experiences. In the West, we value analytic thought.[1] Western researchers in human potential, who are educated in this ideal, aim at making us *better* at analytical thinking. In Japan, where group harmony is valued, there is considerable incentive for human potential research to focus on increasing individuals' ability to blend seamlessly into a group.

In a way, group harmony is valued in Zen. The Zen practitioner is enjoined from distracting his fellows from concentrating on their individual practices. In Zen, as well as in Japanese business, causing a distraction means

---

[1] Among other reasons, because of Descartes' dictum, "I think, therefore I am." Zen practitioners, incidentally, regard Descartes' statement as one of the silliest things they've ever heard.

drawing attention to oneself. This is seen as egoistic exhibitionism, harmful to the group. However, in Zen, the *individual* achieves enlightenment, with the support of the community of seekers, and then as an enlightened being, is beyond the need for social support. In industry, the *group* completes the project, and must maintain its all-important social cohesion in order to tackle the next project. This is a very different paradigm.

Tatsuno's assertion that a return to Zen can make creativity blossom is certainly true in principle. Is it likely in practice? The readings described below provide clues. Widely available current editions are noted in parenthesis.

☯

Miyamoto Musashi, *A Book of Five Rings.* Recently popular among U.S. executives, this short book details the 16th-century sword-master's strategy of conflict. To Musashi, strategy did encompass tactical engagement and follow-up, which is almost the exclusive focus of U.S. business strategy. But readers should note Mushashi's near total strategic emphasis on preliminary groundwork, training, research and planning, which created a context for the engagement that was favorable to the planner. Musashi's emphasis on concentration and training is timeless. However, his modern admirers should realize Musashi's violent orientation elucidates the technique but not the Way. (The Overlook Press, Woodstock, NY, 1982.)

D.T. Suzuki, *Zen and Japanese Culture.* This is the English-language sourcebook, written by the first Zen scholar to live and travel in Europe and the U.S. Suzuki offers little direct advice on Zen practice, concentrating instead on history and doctrine. (Princeton University Press, Princeton, NJ, 1970.)

Eugen Herrigel, *Zen in the Art of Archery.* This book is significant for two reasons. First, because it is one of the earlier accounts by a European studying a Zen art in Japan. Herrigel, a German, studied Zen archery prior to World War II. He then returned to Germany and joined the Nazi party. This is the second point of significance: He produced insightful and beautiful descriptions of Zen pursuit, but he just didn't get it. The book serves to warn us of the danger of partial knowledge, and how easy it is to misinterpret or twist a teaching. (Random House-Vintage Books, 1989.)

Shunryu Suzuki, *Zen Mind, Beginner's Mind.* Named by many as their favorite Zen book. Shunryu, known as Suzuki-Roshi and not to be confused with D.T. Suzuki, wrote in simple language without condescending to his earnest American students. Yet the book is a deep and inspiring introduction to Zen life. (Weatherhill, New York, 1970.)

Peter Matthiessen, *Nine-Headed Dragon River.* Matthiessen is a well-known writer on nature and on the political struggles of native peoples. As the book opens, Matthiessen returns from an assignment in Africa to find three Zen masters waiting in his suburban New York driveway. He is drawn into his wife's Zen study group, ultimately becoming a Zen monk and embarking on pilgrimages to Japan and Tibet. The account of the latter trip provides a behind-the-scenes look at the writing of his best seller *The Snow Leopard.* An absorbing account of the growth of Zen in the U.S., and a readable dose of the history of Zen. (Shambhala Publications, Inc., Boston, ©1985.)

John Stevens, *The Sword of No-Sword: Life of the Master Warrior Tesshu.* Tesshu Yamaoka was one of the architects of the Meiji Restoration. He was also the most celebrated Japanese swordsman since Musashi, and one of the foremost Zen practitioners of his day. Former Japanese Prime Minister Nakasone is a devotee of Yamaoka, and meditates daily at a temple founded by Tesshu. Stevens' biography of Yamaoka illuminates the interaction between Zen and Japanese executive leadership that persists to this day. (Shambhala, Boulder CO, 1984.)

Janwillem Van De Wetering, *The Empty Mirror* and *A Glimpse of Nothingness.* The experiences of a young Dutchman in a Japanese Zen monastery. Readers in their twenties will easily identify with the young Van De Wetering's aspirations and difficulties. The writing is witty and insightful. Van De Wetering later became a writer of murder mysteries. The latter are enjoyable stories, quirky and moody, and they are easy to find in bookstores and libraries. You can have fun identifying the Zen influences in them. (Editions of *Mirror* and *Nothingness* are available through Ballantine and Pocket Books.)

Albert Low, *Zen and Creative Management.* This is the only serious book in print with both words, Zen and management, in the title. So it is a disappointment that reading this difficult book is so unrewarding. Low was a student of Roshi Philip Kapleau, and now heads the Montreal Zen Center. Prior to studying with Kapleau, the bio-blurb tells us, Low was a business executive. But his orientation and writing style is that of a European academic philosopher. The result is heavy reading, in no way reminiscent of the clear, direct and compelling writing of Shunryu Suzuki or Chögyam Trungpa, who, unlike Low, were not writing in their native languages.

His emotional tie to the world of commerce is evident; one might say Low follows Adam Smith in trying to conceive a "commercial philosophy." This book could serve to get liberal arts students interested in management. But there's not much Zen here, not explicitly anyway. Peter Drucker is quoted extensively, and readers would do better to go directly to Drucker.

It's easy to show that things are not simple – that business, for example, cannot be evaluated on the single dimension of profit or shareholder value. It is more difficult to offer a useable alternative concept that encompasses more of the required complexities. Although Low introduces some good distinctions, e.g., "problem" vs. "dilemma," and "important" vs. "urgent," and offers some valuable observations on the creative value of conflicts in organizations, he has not offered such a coherent alternative. (Charles Tuttle & Co., 1993.)

You may enjoy the works of the authors mentioned incidentally above, notably Chögyam Trungpa, *Cutting Through Spiritual Materialism,* Shambhala, Berkeley, 1973, and Philip Kapleau, *The Three Pillars of Zen,* New York, Harper and Row, 1966.

The *Japan Management Review* reports that Japanese firms are nurturing creativity among workers by: (i) emphasizing problem-finding as well as problem solving, and also evaluating and implementing solutions as a routine part of everyone's job; (ii) portraying problems as opportunities rather than as embarrassments; and (iii) increasingly offering employees a choice of job assignments, thus tapping previously unrecognized employee talent.

The Japanese company most identified with an explicit Zen orientation is Kao, a diversified corporation that began as a soap manufacturer. Under the leadership of Zen student Dr. Yoshio Maruta in the 1970s and 80s, Kao gained a reputation as a leader in innovation and ranks high in *Nikkei Business*'s list of excellent companies. The company shares information among employees and outsiders to an exceptional degree, and is a leader in the effective use of information technology – even (and until the mid-1990s this was rare in Japan) among the office and white-collar workforce.

*Many think success and excellence... are the same. They are not. There is
no substitute for excellence, not even success. Success is tricky, perishable,
and often outside our control; the pursuit of success makes a poor
cornerstone, especially for a whole personality. Excellence is dependable,
lasting and largely an issue within our own control; pursuit of excellence, in
and for itself, is the best of foundations.*
- Thomas Boswell

On Mastery

At the universities where I've taught, MBA students are exposed to
the achievements and methods of distinguished businesspeople. Some of these
executives owe their success to dumb luck or unpardonably exploitative
practices. Others have truly mastered the art and science of management.
Sometimes it's hard to tell which, so we carefully use the word "distinguished"
to hedge whether the distinction is of a positive character or otherwise.

Thomas Boswell, author of this chapter's opening quotation and a book
called *The Heart of the Order,* addresses the difference between success and
excellence. George Leonard's short volume *Mastery* pursues the same theme,
warning against "the prevailing bottom-line mentality that puts quick, easy
results ahead of long-term dedication to the journey itself." According to
Leonard, success is characterized by a climactic moment. Its pursuit can lead
only to an addiction to bigger and better climaxes. Mastery, in contrast, is a
never-ending process with many plateaus and local peaks, but no climax or
terminus. The path of mastery is goal-less, and so eliminates the tension between
means and ends. There are no ends in an endless process, and means can only
be defined in terms of ends. Therefore, mastery implies a concentration on the
process itself; a Zen-like experience of the moment, that leads to learning and
self-discipline. Leonard applies the Zen saying, "When you get to the top of
the mountain, keep climbing," to managerial and personal growth.

In an interesting turn for a man who was a focal point for social change
in the 1960s and 70s, Leonard shows how traditional values relate to the
development of mastery. His exposition will touch a chord for American
businesspeople who are starting to look with approval on German and other
apprenticeship programs: "Values were once inculcated through the extended
family, tribal or village elders, sports and games, the apprenticeship system or
traditional schooling, religious training and practice, and spiritual and secular
ceremony." Not to mention the military – *Mastery* also builds on Leonard's
experiences as an Air Force flight instructor in World War II.

A highlight of *Mastery* is Leonard's exposition of homeostasis in organisms and organizations. This is the force that, strangely, must be both yielded to and overcome in order to effect change. "Our body, brain and behavior have a built-in tendency to stay the same within rather narrow limits, and to snap back when changed.... No need here to count the ways organizations and cultures resist change and backslide when change does occur."

Leonard and colleagues interviewed master athletes who credited hard work over raw talent. "I have seen so many baseball players with God-given ability who just didn't want to work," Rod Carew said. "They were soon gone. I've seen others with no ability to speak of who stayed in the big leagues for fourteen or fifteen years." This may be because the talented expect a certain level of performance; the less-talented but persevering, burdened with fewer expectations, will just keep working and improving.

The path of mastery is a joy, not a grind, and Leonard under-emphasizes the importance of play. Play can boost learning and discovery, highlighting areas where mastery is needed. Moreover, fun is an effective motivator. Similarly, he overemphasizes the difficulty of aikido: "I was fortunate in my middle years to have found aikido, a discipline so difficult and resistant to the quick fix that it showed me the plateau in sharp, bold relief.... Many years later I found myself once again in the instructor's role, engaged this time in an art far more subtle and complex ... than flying." If my first aikido teachers had hammered me with the difficulty of the art, I might not have persisted in it! Better to invoke another Zen principle: Refrain from building walls between the ordinary and the extraordinary.

This view of mastery will remind readers of the fabled Japanese practice of "continuous improvement," which business educators contrast with a purported American preference for breakthrough or quantum-leap innovation (though how an affection for breakthroughs, which are rare and cannot be scheduled, jibes with a purported "quick-fix" orientation, is a mystery I've not plumbed). But Leonard is suggesting something far more sophisticated and realistic, something that may be the principal contribution of *Mastery*. Continuous efforts at improvement do not imply continuously improved results; there are plateaus. The plateaus may be preceded by gently upward curves of improvement, and followed by a great leap forward, which may in turn be followed by another long plateau, in a nonlinear progression. On the path of mastery, with the focus on the journey and not on the result, effort is expended at a constant rate, but results are nonlinear and intermittent. George Leonard's view of this process is not only a synthesis of East and West, but a soothing relief for managers frustrated by the apparent contradictions in the continuous-improvement vs. breakthrough debate.

Leonard's books have been sold variously in the sports, education, autobiography, and self-improvement categories. His search for a marketing niche for his writing illustrates the difficulties in presenting master paths, including aikido, to Americans. Aikido is not a sport, not a performing art, but a journey. A student trains not for the winning or for acclaim, but for the training itself. The same applies, of course, to management. Conventional rewards (money, job advancement) usually follow as a secondary effect of cultivating excellence. The manager who regards these as nothing out of the ordinary, who keeps on training, finds happiness.

Mastery is organized in bullet points, with all bullets brought together for quick reference in a summary chapter. This makes the slim volume an easy reference for readers to whom its ideas are new and strange. A mix of philosophical discourse and practical tips for readers wishing to start or continue the journey of mastery, *Mastery* lists pitfalls along the path of mastery, tells how to choose teachers, and helps diagnose personality types and their unique approaches to learning. A forthcoming re-release promises to eliminate the editing errors that mar the first edition.

In a cover blurb, management consultant Tom Peters says *Mastery* cured him of his orientation to the quick fix. Readers of Peters' columns will recognize that this was no mean feat.

Past seventy years of age and still teaching aikido in California, George Leonard is a true embodiment of mastery. His message is important: "If winning is the only thing, then practice, discipline, conditioning and character are nothing." Use this book as an introduction to one of the pioneers of the transformation of American consciousness, and as an invaluable manual for your own transformation.

Test

> *Resistance...is proportionate to the size and speed of [a] change, not to whether the change is a favorable or unfavorable one. If an organizational... reform meets tremendous resistance, it is because it's either a tremendously bad idea or a tremendously good idea. Trivial change, bureaucratic meddling, is much easier to accept, and that's one reason why you see so much of it.*
>
> *... [An] entire system has to change when any part of it changes. So don't be surprised if... people you love start covertly or overtly undermining your self-improvement. It's not that they wish you harm, it's just homeostasis at work....*
>
> - George Leonard

Test your progress, and test your practice. Are you honing your consciousness? Are you progressing satisfactorily, thanks to a good teacher and your own sincere effort? Or is an illegitimate teacher flattering your ego, emptying your wallet, and wasting your time?

When a credentialed teacher says you've passed your Zen koan, got an A in your MBA ethics course, or advanced to your next belt in martial art, it is probably a sign of progress. When you have won the business plan competition and gained funding for your plan; when you have met your weight loss goal and kept your exercise resolutions; or when you have forgiven a political nemesis without allowing him to take advantage of you again – you may be pretty sure this is real progress.

There is a danger, in that a master practice removes you, for a while, from your habitual social interactions, and requires you to focus on matters other than the latest headline news. What is the difference between progress on a path of non-attachment, and simply sinking into apathy? We might joke that in the latter case, you wouldn't care about the answer. But the true answer is that only tests can tell. Without tests, there is no master path. Look into yourself; *you* know whether you've done a good job in meeting your latest challenge.

This section describes challenging situations typical of those a conscious manager may face, and explores how the conscious manager responds.

I had joined a pilgrimage to the East, seemingly a definite and single pilgrimage – but in reality, this expedition to the East was not only mine and now; this procession of believers and disciples had always and incessantly been moving toward the East. Throughout the centuries... each member, each group... was only a wave in the eternal stream of human beings, of the eternal striving of the human spirit toward the East, toward Home.
- Hermann Hesse, The Journey to the East.

So You're Going to Learn Japanese

Are you considering learning Japanese? Are you required to learn the language as a member of a joint venture team? In this chapter you'll find some practical tips. If you are not studying Japanese, read on anyway. These pages give you the conscious manager's framework for attending to the communications styles and strategies of others.

First, the good news. Japanese is fairly easy to pronounce. The five vowel sounds are pronounced much as they are in Spanish; if you can pronounce Spanish, you can pronounce Japanese. The consonants are also fairly easy for an English speaker, making Japanese a much easier exercise for the Anglophone tongue than, say, French. As with French, though, you will have to practice a great deal to be able to speak with the rapidity that is customary among native speakers.

More good news. Gender, plural, conjugation, case and tense are very simple in the Japanese language. You are also relieved of having to remember which syllable the accent is on, because for the most part every syllable in a word is stressed equally. Surprisingly, this does not make the language sound monotonous (except when Japanese officials are giving speeches). With a good ear and careful listening, you can pick up and imitate the more frequently used patterns of vocal dynamics, which are not subject to formal rules.

As if to make up for the relative neglect of tense and conjugation, Japanese contains a fearsome device called *keigo*. Keigo is the inflection of verbs to indicate degree of politeness or deference to a person of different rank. Keigo is next to impossible for a non-Japanese to master, because of its many gradations of politeness, and because as a *gaijin* (foreigner) your rank in Japanese society is ambiguous at best. I'll conclude this essay with a few words on how to deal with that, but first more on language learning.

The basic linguistic skills are listening, speaking, reading and writing. Subject to what I've said above, speaking and listening in Japanese present no unique problems. Reading and writing are another story!

There is no Japanese alphabet. In lieu of an alphabet, Japanese uses syllabaries (*kana*) in which each symbol stands for a syllable, and ideographs (*kanji*). Each symbol in the *hiragana* and *katakana* syllabaries represents a syllable. This distinguishes Japanese from English and other languages that use an alphabet, in which there is a distinct symbol for each phoneme. There are about fifty or fifty-five symbols in each of the kana, depending how you count minor variations. Because the two kana are alternate ways of symbolizing the same set of syllables, this means there are only about fifty syllables that it is possible to pronounce in Japanese! All Japanese words are composed of syllables drawn from this set of fifty.

In general, hiragana is used for native Japanese words, and katakana for foreign borrowings, for emphasis or onomatopoeia, and in books for small children who've not yet learned hiragana. However, I recently saw a sign in Tokyo that made a transliteration of "bakery" in hiragana, and the ubiquitous "karaoke" sign (karaoke is composed of the native Japanese word for "empty" and an almost unrecognizable adaptation of the English word "orchestra") is rendered in katakana. Over the years, I've noticed more and more English words have been borrowed, and more katakana is seen than previously. You will also see Japanese names or words written in *Romaji* (Roman characters) in certain situations, and there are a couple of standard systems for such transliteration.

Japanese text is a mixture of kana and *kanji*. The kanji are adapted from Chinese characters, and the basic principle is that a single kanji ideograph represents a single idea or name. You must be able to recognize about 2,000 kanji before you can read and comprehend even a simple newspaper article in Japanese! This number does not include kanji for proper names (people and places), of which there are thousands more.

Those who are mathematically inclined can see that building a rich language like Japanese from fifty-some syllables means a choice must be made. Either the language must have a heck of a lot of really long words, or a heck of a lot of homonyms. Japanese has chosen the latter course, with many words and kanji having identical pronunciations. Context usually suffices to indicate meaning, but you may travel to Japan and be treated to the comical sight of two Japanese in conversation tracing kanji in the air with their fingers to resolve the ambiguity in a spoken sentence.

The number of homonyms is truly excessive when one needs such stratagems. One result is that the Japanese are distressed by puns, and do not find them the least bit funny when used in conversation or low humor. Until recently, puns were found primarily in classical poetry, where they illustrated the beauty of ambiguity and the poet's mastery of language. That's why it's remarkable that Japanese advertisements have now adopted the American practice of punning slogans. We'll see whether this sells product there or not.

Although I have forgotten the pronunciation of many of the kanji I've learned, I do recognize their meaning when I see them. People from China or Korea can recognize the meaning of a kanji character even if they do not know the Japanese pronunciation. This implies one may learn to read kanji for meaning, or pronunciation (reading aloud). To recognize meaning only is certainly easier, but I encourage learning pronunciation if one intends to be anything but a casual translator. Writing is also easier than it used to be. This is because of the proliferation of Japanese word processors. These wonderful machines accept input in hiragana or Romaji, and respond with menus of the most common corresponding kanji. Writing by hand still requires memorizing the position of each squiggle and curlicue in each kanji, and, if you are to be a decent calligrapher, the order in which each stroke is put to paper.

> **Management Challenge:** *Economic Competitiveness.* The interesting – and economically important – point is that Japanese schools emphasize reading and writing English, with little or no instruction in speaking. Seitaro, an upper-level salaryman, has terrible difficulty pronouncing English, but like most of his colleagues, he can comprehend written English without much trouble. This means it is a courtesy to him to put important business communications in writing (assuming his English is better than your Japanese), using face time for enjoyable personal bonding. Joe, one of Seitaro's American suppliers, makes a point of doing this. Joe knows this bonding will also increase the chances of a common understanding and interpretation of the documents, and make contract disputes less likely.

The Japanese educational emphasis also means that Japan has millions of people who can read English-language business and technical literature, and the U.S., for example, has but a handful who can read Japanese journals and reports. So, even though the task is daunting, it is worthwhile to make it a goal to learn to read Japanese.

Some help is available that was not there in the past. Many software products are on the commercial or shareware markets, though in my experience none make a significant difference in speed of learning. As your learning advances, do subscribe to *Mangajin,* a great magazine that uses comic strips, advertising, and current events to impart practical and memorable language tips. Kenkyusha's neat *Japanese-English Learner's Dictionary* provides sample sentences for each word entry. Japanese is such an idiomatic language that a word used in the wrong context is meaningless, and so most dictionaries are almost useless; I've hesitated to use a newly learned word until I've heard someone else use it. The new Kenkyusha solves that problem, and also serves the traditional function of connecting the reader with intriguing new words. Two of my favorites, perhaps because of the way they just bounce out of the mouth, are *tokidoki* ("sometimes"), and *kokonotsu* ("nine").

Try to use the idiomatic nature of the language to gain competence in communication, not just in vocabulary. Because each word and phrase is tied to a cultural context, you can learn about the Japanese people's history and motivation by looking into the situations in which they use that word or phrase. For example, readers of this book will recognize that the phrase *sannen ni mo ishi no ue* ("three more years on a stone"), signifying patience, is a reference to sitting zazen on a hard cushion. Though English phrases are often more portable from one situation to another (and this might be one reason why English is so widely used around the world), your Japanese language experience might help you see that certain English phrases are more idiomatic than you thought. If you have had difficulties conveying your thoughts to non-American or non-native English speakers, this might be the reason! In any case, paying attention to idiom is a part of paying attention to context, and it makes you a more conscious communicator.

Professor Hal Boyles of St. Edward's University in Austin has developed a system for teaching technical Japanese that will enable a student with no prior background in the language to grasp the gist of a Japanese journal article in his or her technical discipline in one hundred hours of classroom study. This focused instruction concentrates on basics of grammar and sentence structure, learning the kana for the connective particle parts of speech, then moves on to kanji and kanji compounds common to most scientific and technical areas, and finally to constructs specific to the students' own technical disciplines. Jim Davis at University of Wisconsin, Michio Tsutsui at University of Washington and others have made great strides in making technical Japanese language resources available via Internet and distance learning.

● *Tool: Keigo.* The newsstands are full of books on how to "get along in Japan." Many of them try to prescribe how many degrees one should bow in different situations – as if anyone could memorize this. Bowing, and keigo, assume you are part of Japanese society, which is generally not true for non-Japanese. My advice is to choose one very polite form of verb usage and stick with it. (Ask your Japanese teacher for his or her opinion.) Age has a lot to do with social status. As you associate in social situations with Japanese of your own age, you will easily pick up the more informal verb forms. Should you bow in Japanese social and business situations? I see it this way: Shaking hands is very awkward and alien for a Japanese. Yet we appreciate it when he or she attempts to shake hands with us. I think a bow that is neither too deep nor to curt is a nice reciprocal attempt to bridge the culture gap, and will be received the same way we receive the handshake.

If you are not to be a serious student of the language, learn some elementary phrases for social and business situations. Pronunciation is easy, and you can build a small arsenal of useful phrases without much difficulty. As long as your language skills remain at tourist level, your Japanese acquaintances will think of you as a quaint foreigner, and extend every possible courtesy to you. Paradoxically, if your Japanese becomes fluent, the question of your place in Japanese social hierarchies comes to the forefront, causing your Japanese friends much confusion and distress. In that case, except with your closest friends, your best strategy may be to keep your ears open and your mouth shut.

When you speak with a Japanese, "unranked" as you are, he or she will be looking not for adherence to formulas, but for certain human qualities in you – sincerity, warmth, courtesy, and purpose. Make sure you display these things.

Our understanding of what globalization is and what it will do is still primitive.
- Bradford De Long

The Way of Buddha
is to know yourself.
To know yourself
is to forget yourself.
To forget yourself
is to be enlightened by all things.
- Dogen

Icons and Institutions – Views from Seattle and Tokyo

The 1999 anti-globalization protests in Seattle have become an icon. Years later, the mere mention of the city's name evokes images of civil disobedience, police over-reaction, strange political bedfellows, and confrontation over abstract, badly understood issues.

As the dust settled in Seattle, World Trade Organization delegates, protesters, and press wrangled about who won and who lost. WTO opponents and proponents did their best to portray free trade as a clear choice between jobs and consumer prices. The delegates, refusing to consider environmental and human rights in this round, ensured the one-dimensional character of the debate.

To the conscious manager, important issues are never one-dimensional. The conscious manager suspects that anyone painting a question black and white is trying to direct our attention away from other concerns. *Something* made a variety of Americans, from the political right and left, march together in Seattle. That something wasn't jobs and prices, important as they are. Many and complex fears sent citizens to the barricades in November, 1999. What were they? The free trade issue is surrounded by international intrigue and powerful historical forces, the stuff of novels. We must look to Japan again for some of the clues.

The globalizing economy challenges our fear of change and of losing control. It challenges our focus, that is, our ability to withstand the attempts of others to misdirect us. It also challenges our icons, and the discomfort we feel when we are confused about their true status. Should we compare the Seattle protests to the Boston Tea Party? Do we really honor the memory of the Boston tea protest, or is that just so much pabulum for school children?

And most important, the new economy challenges us to ask the fundamental question, "How shall we live?" What kinds of civil institutions will we keep, which will we discard, and what new ones will we build? Are we capable of making these decisions in a conscious way?

☯

We can find answers by looking at the institutions that shape our lives, and how they became what they are.

Which is the oldest: democracy, the nation-state, or the corporation? That's easy – everyone knows democracy dates to ancient Athens. For millennia after Athens, people lived in city-states (Athens was one), kingdoms, empires, colonies and so forth, their boundaries set by continual war and shifting alliances. It was only after World War I that the modern nation-state – governed by its natives, participating in international discourse, and with boundaries relatively fixed and recognized by international convention – came into being.

What about corporations? As late as 1900, there were only about thirty of them in the United States. Historically, corporations were granted at the pleasure of the sovereign, for limited purposes. Corporations sometimes became as powerful as governments, for example the Hudson Bay company in Canada, and United Fruit in Central America. But these were essentially colonial situations, and the post-World War I nation-state seemed incompatible with the idea of corporations as governing bodies. Indeed, acknowledging the danger of expansionist corporations, the U.S. occupying forces dismantled the Japanese *zaibatsu* industrial conglomerates after World War II, and President Eisenhower warned us about the military-industrial complex.

Japan became a nation-state earlier than most European countries. Historically, Japan fit most of the criteria just mentioned, except that until Admiral Perry, there was little international discourse. "Japan still has a feudal mind-set," says Tokyo University's Kenichi Arai, referring to a tradition of fealty to *daimyo* warlords and to the emperor rather than to the nation. Japan also suffers from defining itself in ethnic terms, a malady that is corroding nation-states like Canada and Israel, not to mention Yugoslavia.

The U.S. was one of the few modern nation-states that was neither a historical-geographical accident nor a creation of external political force. America was designed from within. Japan has a national creation myth with a full cast of deities, but in America's creation mythos the central characters are the Declaration of Independence, the Constitution and the Bill of Rights. Never feudal, America's society has always been mobile. We demanded government protection from traveling snake oil scams and from the likes of Harold Hill the Music Man. We demanded it and got it, and in a dialectic that looks inevitable in hindsight, the Harold Hills, and their more honest cousins, had to protect themselves from abuses of the government protection. They formed the limited-liability corporations that are everywhere today. As legal quasi-persons, corporations cannot vote in political elections, but can lobby and make political contributions to further their interests.

Whose interests are those? We Americans are the corporations and they are us. We are employed by them, we consume their products, and, through our investments or pension plans, we own them. This is unlike the Japanese, whose personal savings are mostly in their postal savings system. Individual Americans are also voters, and still expect the corporations to abide by the law of the sovereign – which is also us. We are increasingly at risk of being disappointed in this expectation.

Free trade agreements like NAFTA, the World Trade Organization (WTO), and the Multilateral Agreement on Investments (MAI) subordinate government power to corporate decisions. Most of us would think of this, to use the mildest possible language, as putting the cart before the horse. If these trade agreements proceed, the United States moves from a liberal-statist to a corporatist country in less than fifty years. How would such a shift affect our lives? I'll frame this discussion in terms of MAI, because of all trade proposals to date, MAI would imply the most extreme changes to the status quo. A study of Japan helps us understand what life might be like in the corporatist regime that would result from MAI.

Trade and Capital

Industries use land, labor, and capital to produce goods and services. Nowadays people add "technology" to the list of inputs. Capital (money) moves more freely than ever before. With negligible exceptions, land stays in one place. Labor obviously does not cross borders freely, except within the European Community, and even affluent knowledge workers face formidable visa problems when travelling for work purposes between the other nations of the world. On the output side, goods move reasonably freely except for various tariffs and sanctions. When services are provided in face-to-face settings, movement of services is restricted the same way labor movement is restricted. Online and telemarketing services cross borders with much greater ease. Only two of the five or six factors of trade actually move freely, so "free trade," in the WTO sense, seems an exaggeration.

According to the renowned scholar and commentator Noam Chomsky, "Financial capital can impose the social policies it chooses on governments and can punish those that deviate.... for example, efforts to stimulate the economy or to create full employment or ... other [inefficient] purposes can be terminated and punished simply by flight of capital, which these days even rich and powerful states can't withstand." In 1944, forty-some nations with war-torn but still viable economies sent delegates to Bretton Woods, New Hampshire, to devise international financial policies for a post-war world. The Bretton Woods monetary agreement regulated capital very strictly. The economies of its signatories (including the U.S. and Japan) were characterized by high GNP growth, high productivity growth, and expansion of the social contract, if also by low profits. The U.S. and other countries abandoned the Bretton Woods regime in the 1970s; the result was lower growth and higher profits. Japan kept up the high-regulation/high-growth/low-profit regime, ironically making that country look aggressive to American eyes.

In good times, people prefer open trade, says *The Economist*. However, the magazine's 1999 survey shows that U.S. consumers, pleased with the current state of our economy, favor protectionism over free trade by about twenty percentage points. Japanese consumers, hungry for cheaper imports, prefer free trade by about the same margin. *The Economist* also notes that the profitability of companies is shrinking, and *Business Week* talks about "the deteriorating quality of corporate earnings," a reference to an increasing use of misleading bookkeeping. These contradictions have spurred corporations to lobby for trade agreements that give them greater latitude.

The MAI

A treaty that is as pro-corporation as the MAI naturally generates a lot of wild and ungrammatical populist response. A more literate but no less impassioned viewpoint comes from Chomsky, and the Western Governors' Association published a sober but still critical analysis of the treaty. Still more responsible opposition comes from the *Christian Science Monitor*: "This treaty will transform government of, by, and for the people into government of, by, and for the corporations."

Here is a short summary of the MAI, as gleaned from these sources: Companies may not be kept from moving their assets or profits across national borders. Trans-national corporations (TNCs) can sue governments, but not vice versa. (This is deeply cynical. When the main thrust of the MAI is to undermine governments, why does the treaty recognize governments as legitimate targets of litigation? For one reason only: Governments collect taxes, so that's where the money is.) All TNCs, no matter where incorporated, are free to bid for privatized government enterprises. No quid pro quo can be required from companies when states or cities offer tax incentives for location, and indeed such incentives may be banned. Signatory governments will be forced to deregulate all industries that ask for it.

The MAI opposes any government taking or giving that "distorts" private market allocation of capital. Companies may not be compelled to use domestic content, transfer new technology, or export a certain level of manufactured goods. There would be no exceptions for health, safety, or environmental standards, or local cultural content. Only a crisis of public order or international peace and security would allow governments to act without regard to investor protection.

A Canadian book about the treaty is number seven on that country's best-seller list, five provinces refused to participate in the treaty by declaring themselves MAI-free zones, and the Canadian government announced it cannot sign the current treaty. In France, tens of thousands of protesters took to the streets, forcing the French government to call for a re-negotiation of the treaty. In New Zealand, the parliament exploded into fury upon discovering the government had been secretly negotiating the MAI.

Because of widespread popular resistance to the treaty, MAI negotiations have stalled as of the date of this writing, and given the failure of WTO's Seattle meeting, may not resume for some time. But this has not stopped officials of the European Commission and the Japanese Ministry of International Trade and Industry (MITI) from continuing to speak in favor of the treaty's provisions.

Anyone who believes Americans' only legitimate civic impulses are soldiering and policing will love MAI.

Japan as Bellwether

Can Japan be called corporatist? Absolutely! The press often speaks of "Japan, Inc." From its imperial expansionism in the first half of the century, driven by its military-industrial complex, to today's disempowered Japanese consumers and the neon ad extravaganzas in Ginza and Kabukicho, the corporate influence on Japanese life seems overwhelming. Religion is not a major preoccupation of the Japanese, and governments rise and fall with frequency, but the companies and their *keiretsu* groups persist. The increased international expansion of Japanese firms lessens the control of the government ministries over their activities. Japanese corporations' influence and power continue to increase.

What aspects of Japanese corporatism foreshadow what the U.S. would be like under an extreme free trade agreement (FTA) like the MAI? Some of them are Japan's:

- Emphasis on rote learning in school. Americans now at least pretend that public schools teach children to be responsible world citizens, and not just cogs in the corporate machine. In Japan it is more explicit that only the elite will engage in policy making. Schooling for the remainder need be nothing more than job training. Japanese, while not the first people one would think of as exemplars of creativity and statesmanship, are well-informed and think in terms of their national interest. Americans' more liberal education has resulted in a populace that is self-absorbed and generally ill-informed about world affairs.
- Horizontal and vertical integration (cross-ownership) of companies. FTA negotiators trumpet the need for "confidence and stability." A curmudgeon would read this as confidence for investors and stability of the labor force. Full Japanese-style cross-ownership, while currently illegal in the U.S., does serve both of those goals.

- Vulnerability to crashes in the economies of neighboring countries. When regional markets are isolated by trade barriers, a crash in one need not affect another. When the whole world is one market, all regions prosper or crash together.
- Weakness in entrepreneurship and venture capital. Rote learning doesn't promote thinking-out-of-the-box entrepreneurship. The kind of stability sought by large corporations causes each entrepreneurial nail that sticks up to be hammered down. The strong Japanese need to be part of a group deters lone-wolf entrepreneurship.
- Secrecy, with company records not easily accessible. There is no need to report to individual shareholders because there are so few individual shareholders. The press plays no role in building shareholder confidence, so why tell the press anything?

What current features of Japanese corporatism would *not* characterize the U.S. under MAI?

Certainly not Japan's "statist capitalism," with industry taking direction from government ministries. First, the FTAs' primary effect is to weaken the ability of governments to regulate trade. Second, most Japanese personal savings are in Ministry of Finance postal deposit accounts, not with private brokers. The U.S. has no tradition of government as savings bank, with the exception of the involuntary social security system. Third, Japan's slowness to adapt to office automation and the Internet. America has led the way in rapid adoption of these technologies. Fourth, Japan's well-educated workforce. While Japan has a well-established school system and near-universal literacy, the quality of U.S. schools and students, and the rate at which kids drop out or are incarcerated, are alarming. And finally, corporate farming has not dominated Japanese agriculture, as it does in the U.S. Individual Japanese farmers exert great voting power in their nation's democracy, and counterbalance urban industrial-oriented voting. This force is not counted among America's checks and balances.

Some other areas are harder to predict. Japan does not have a social welfare structure like the U.S. or western Europe. Would U.S. welfare be eliminated under MAI as a "market distortion" (WTO's phrase)? If so, it would be destabilizing, as large numbers of poor unemployed hit the streets. Maintaining welfare, while stabilizing, hurts investor confidence. The Japanese construction industry is favored by massive public works spending. It leads to corruption, but also to the infrastructure that supports economic growth. How would infrastructure get built under MAI? Rabid free-traders tend to forget they went to public schools and transport their products via public roads and airports.

Calling Japan a bellwether of corporatism is not a criticism of Japan. In the devastation following their World War II defeat, Japan had no choice but to sacrifice consumer sovereignty for maximum economic growth. America in the prosperous 2000s has no such excuse.

As these paragraphs show, different histories and social customs mean life in the U.S. under extreme free trade could be much worse than in Japan.

Corporatism and Scientific Progress

Today, new product lines can be devised cheaply by combining knowledge from different fields, different companies, different industries, and different countries. "Technological fusion" –°combining existing ideas and technologies – can generate profits for decades to come, even with no new advances in basic science.

This may reinforce the smugness of certain scientists about the advanced state of knowledge that has led to published discussion of the end of science. One thinks twice before disagreeing with a Richard Feynman or a Stephen Hawking, but the "end of science" is a foolish notion. Consider the as-yet undiscovered "dark matter" that is said to make up the bulk of the universe's mass. People who have misplaced 90% of the universe's matter should not be saying they're close to knowing all there is to know! Talk about the end of science plays into the hands of those who would limit the freedom of ideas.

Nobel Laureate Richard Feynman noted that Soviet Russia and Nazi Germany both showed impressive advances in technology, but that due to the excessive official influence of Lysenko in Russia, and Hitler's glorification of the supposed occult history of the Germans, and the general suppression of new ideas and their expression in both regimes, science did not advance notably in either. Modern science dates from Galileo, whose work was not exactly embraced by the then all-powerful arbiter of ideas, the Catholic church.

The recent increase in Nobel prizes and basic research in Japan seems inconsistent with the notion of corporatist restriction of the flow of ideas. However, only 14% of total 1998 public and private Japanese research expenditure was on basic research, compared to as high as 64% in the U.S. One cannot say broadly that corporatism and so-called free trade are anti-innovation. R&D expenditure, though, is generally associated with long-term growth, rather than with the short-term profits that impel corporations to seek deregulation.

Large companies say they want to liberalize capital flows. That makes their own stock more vulnerable to disinvestment when the company misses a quarterly target. They cut the R&D budget to make the quarterly return look better. Meanwhile, government-sponsored research, condemned as a "market distortion," has dried up and is no longer available to industry. With no innovation in the pipeline, next year's corporate bottom line looks even worse. What kind of madness is this?

Ironically, free trade is touted as a spur to innovation, because international price pressures on inefficient industries can force them to re-invent themselves. In today's world of Silicon Valley style entrepreneurship, innovation is the core culture of the small, fast-growing firms that are adding most of the new jobs in the U.S. The innovation culture is driven by technological fusion, not by price pressure. In other words, the Seattle WTO meeting may easily have been a lot of sound and fury about something that, at bottom, doesn't make business sense.

Management Challenge: Policy in a new world order. Minoru is a cabinet official in a powerful Japanese ministry. His salary is modest compared to that of his U.S. counterpart Richard, but his job perks include a car and driver and a substantial entertainment allowance. The allowance leads visitors to think Minoru lives the high life, but in fact he is hard-pressed to afford imported goods for his home. He is privately embarrassed about his role in restricting imports of ski wax from the U.S.; he had to tell Richard, with a straight face, that Japanese snow is different and foreign wax does not work well on Japanese ski slopes. Richard wants U.S. companies to be able to export more freely to Japan, but he and Minoru consider it their job to negotiate these openings. Neither Richard nor Minoru wants a supra-governmental body like WTO to usurp their countries' sovereign prerogatives in this matter.

As career bureaucrats, both men know that to understand political pressures they must "follow the money." They know investors wish to enjoy the best financing opportunities no matter where on the planet these might be, especially if governments can be made to protect the invested capital against downside risk. These investors have supported the political careers of the elected officials to whom Richard and Minoru report. These officials now support blanket free trade and capital protection agreements and want these agreements to be overseen by supra-national bodies like WTO.

Minoru and Richard know the issue should not be decided on the basis of campaign contributions. They do not have the data they need to decide it on a factual basis, and they know that if they fail to keep building their power base, they will have no ability to decide the matter when better information does come along.

Both men are skilled at bamboozling elected bosses who may not be around four years from now. As conscious managers, they use all the methods at their command, from press leaks to official obfuscation, to keep the situation fluid until the hoped-for time when solid data will allow them to say more confidently that trade and capital liberalization is good or bad for American and Japanese citizens.

Trade and High-Tech

According to Michael Porter of Harvard, "companies' ability to source capital, goods, information, and technology from around the world... should diminish the role of location in competition." Competitive advantage, Porter says, does not rest any longer on driving down input costs, but rather on making more productive use of inputs, which requires continual innovation. He notes the role of location *is* important, then, insofar as geographical clusters of industries, especially technology-intensive industries, offer conditions conducive to innovation. Market, technical and competitive information builds up within a cluster, and local businesses have preferred access to it. In addition, personal relationships and community ties engender trust and help information flow. Clusters thrive because of access to public resources, and companies "must engage locally, fostering good relationships with local government, schools, utilities, etc." Clusters arise and can flourish because of the special nature of the local population, the terrain, or the infrastructure.

Porter's argument is correct as far as it goes, but the new FTAs dictate the availability of inputs, the disposability of outputs, and even the viability of industrial clusters. Under MAI, no quid-pro-quo corporate performance requirements will be allowed in exchange for tax incentives, reducing the ability of localities to encourage cluster growth. Those of us who have witnessed the successes of public-private partnerships like enterprise zones and university new business incubators must be skeptical about extreme FTAs. The growing technopolis movement has many regions trying to build competitive and sustainable industry clusters, using exactly the tools that would be outlawed by MAI.

Japan's advanced industries are clustered not because of the natural advantages of regions, but because they have been government-driven and must be close to the seats of power. As FTAs decouple industry from government, the rationale for this clustering disappears, and Japanese companies will disperse. In America, cities will watch powerlessly as their clusters dissipate.

We have met our rescuers, and they are us.

I first went to Japan in 1975, before the "Japanese quality miracle" had visibly affected U.S. industry, and when the yen was four hundred to the dollar. In those days, Americans still went to Japan as tourists, not as industrial pilgrims. I understood, though, that I was looking at the future. It was antiseptic, corporatist, and stifling. In terms of urban crowding and the social, infrastructural and architectural ways of accommodating a dense population, Tokyo's ways of coping seemed both sensible and inevitable. I was too optimistic about the "inevitable" part. In the ensuing twenty-plus years, U.S. cities did not become more like Tokyo, but rather in their squalor, lawlessness, shrunken tax base, and pollution evolved into free-standing third world countries.

Both extremes have unattractive features. How to ensure a happy medium? The answer is us. When employers oppressed labor, we formed labor unions. When the advertising machine turned us into consumers, we formed consumer unions. Now, when PACs and religious blocs control Congress, we must exercise our rights as citizens and voters. And if MAI removes that sovereignty from our hands, we must exercise our rights as stockholders. It places great demands on our character to play our many roles as producer, consumer, breadwinner, stockholder, and citizen. Only conscious managers can achieve this.

When the cold war ended, it seemed that the difference between the kinds of capitalism practiced in the U.S. and Japan, ignored during the grand conflict between capitalism and communism, would become new arenas of disputation. Any conflict between flavors of capitalism now seems lost in the crisis of post-cold-war conservatism and a confused religious millennialism that both anticipates apocalypse and applies the language of good and evil to the economic debate. It now seems that democracy, federalism, and the nation-state face greater risks than capitalism does. Perhaps this shouldn't surprise us, as capitalism predates democracy, the nation-state, and the corporation.

The Economist uses the word "liberalism" in connection with free trade. Another writer points out that conservatives, ostensibly dedicated to the preservation of traditional values, also seem dedicated to corporations that tend to "chew up every precious thing that stand in their way, including small towns, small farms, old institutions, and you." Right-wing ultra-nationalists and left-wing labor unionists found common ground in Seattle. Both groups believe what parents and teachers said about our ancestors' sacrifices for democracy and independence. We cannot rely on old categories of left and right to resolve free trade issues, but decisions must be made nonetheless.

As I noted at the beginning of this chapter, the dialectic of protection for all parties gives rise to agents and counter-agents. Japan provides clues about how the dialectic might play out. Japanese corporations have perfected the use of *sokaiya,* tough guys who prevent stockholders from having their say at annual meetings. At a time when economic and social initiatives are occurring more and more at regional rather than at national levels, the WTO aims to have nations as member signatories, making its whole thrust appear old-fashioned. Globalization and regionalization are both powerful forces in the year 2002, and WTO addresses, imperfectly, only one of these. The corrosion of nation-states may advance further if regions can preserve their economic development prerogatives only by seceding from their parent nations and from WTO.

The conscious manager cleaves to lifelong learning, and NAFTA-related job losses should jolt everyone into an adult-education class. I am very fond of the U.S. Constitution, but my training tells me not to deify it or identify with it. We honor America's founding fathers and others who made great sacrifices for the nation, but we don't owe them a defense of the Constitution, and we are not compelled to do things the way they did. Secret FTA negotiations put our sovereignty and democratic processes at risk. Conscious managers will oppose them, support them, or ignore them based on values and multi-dimensional analysis, not on knee-jerk constitutionalism.

We have uncovered the real motivating forces behind resistance to free trade. It was not the aim of this chapter to argue for or against free trade. Indeed, it is too soon to decide. The issues and the feasible alternative actions are not yet defined with enough clarity. As Berkeley economist Bradford De Long says, "Our understanding of what globalization is and what it will do is still primitive." Only a manager who is overly proud of his forcefulness, or overconfident of his intuition – or impatient, or caving in to external pressure – would make a for-or-against decision under such circumstances.

The conscious manager will choose the right path at the right time, seeing the big picture, using the systems approach, looking compassionately from the eyes of both proponents and opponents, learning from but not clinging to historical lessons, and using all the tools at hand – voting, lobbying, investing, and even picketing– to pursue the chosen path. Until then, "controlling loosely," a rare and difficult skill, is the conscious manager's best contribution.

❦

Tool: *Using all you have.* Two anecdotes will illustrate this trait of the conscious manager.

In the 1980s, company software developers called on my department to solve a problem in computer graphics. We had to use methods of trigonometry, analytic geometry, and plane geometry to find the pixel coordinates of the desired screen images. The software developers, both mathematics Ph.D.s, were surprised that we found a solution. "We tried to do it all analytically," they said – whatever that means! All the tools needed to solve it were high school-level math, but the trick lay in combining several tools and methods. The developers had been trained in, and got stuck in, a single methodology, crimping their ability to solve problems.

Some months later, I gave a public aikido demonstration at the Plaza of the Americas in San Antonio. In it, I took on multiple attackers while blindfolded. Someone taped the exhibition, and when Toyoda Sensei saw the video, he bawled me out. "Use everything you got!" he told me. Playing with a handicap, as it were, is okay in private practice, and useful for convincing yourself you can do it. Doing it in public is just showing off, unbecoming a conscious manager.

If you went to business school, you were taught certain techniques.

But you are still a human being. You have access to those techniques, but also to your artistic, rhetorical, analytical, athletic, research, and interpersonal talents. And the list doesn't stop there! The conscious manager does not define herself by a menu of professional tools. The conscious manager feels free to draw on any of her human talents to solve whatever problem is at hand.

My senior editor at *Technological Forecasting & Social Change,* Hal Linstone, advocates using "multiple perspectives" to solve management problems. The title of his book, *The Unbounded Mind,* suggests the Zen view of non-attachment to specific perspectives.

Q Many organizational theorists like to look at problems from different "frames," usually the personal frame, the organizational frame and the socio-political frame. Is that what you're advising?

A All the frames are useful, but only if concern for the enlightenment of individuals remains paramount. "Using all you have" means not taking a restrictive view of what it means to be a professional. If dealing with a management issue requires you to give a persuasive presentation *and* take a group of employees on a team-building ropes course *and* gin up a financial plan *and* counsel a few subordinates individually *and* design a community service program *and* chat up a Congressman's staffer *and* take off your jacket and unclog the toilets, then you must not think that any of these tasks is outside your proper range of actions.

Of course you may delegate some of them, but never think it is improper to conceive them and set their implementation in motion. If in order to make your point, you need to hang upside down from the second-story window ledge, cook a meal, sing karaoke, shave your head, plant a tree, or do both parts of the balcony scene from *Romeo and Juliet* – don't hesitate!

Aiki is not an art to fight with or to defeat an enemy. It is a Way in which to harmonize all people into one family.
- Morihei Ueshiba

Why did Bodhidharma travel to the East?
- Zen koan

An Open Letter to Molly Ivins

Ms. Ivins' April 13, 1998 syndicated newspaper column opposed increasing the number of H-1B visas issued to foreign knowledge workers, an issue of great concern primarily to high technology companies. Later in the year, Congress did authorize the increase.

My response to Ms. Ivins' column respected her concern for displacing American workers, but pointed out that Americans' jobs are not threatened by either temporary or permanent immigration of highly educated professionals. I include the letter in this book because it reflects so many of the concerns of the conscious manager that are listed in the book's introduction: the emphasis on education, the rejection of facile liberal/conservative labels, the respect for the contributions of many countries' emigrants to the U.S.' quality of life, and the attempt, unfortunately incomplete in this case, to find a systemic solution to the problem.

A few technology executives have told me they "just can't believe" that immigration of professionals could be an issue with anyone. These execs need to develop a sense of context in order to become conscious managers, especially a sense of the political and public relations contexts of their business. Molly's column showed a bias against the high technology industry (perhaps she would not have written it if it were a more traditional industry hurting for employees), and Congress wasn't terribly sympathetic to the industry in their H-1B deliberations. After the Microsoft antitrust decision, technology firms will begin to take the trouble to build relationships in Washington D.C. If they would run some ads showing how my Mom and Dad in Illinois exchange email and digital photos with my kids in Oregon, Molly Ivins and others might see how high technology can restore family closeness and some other traditions we had feared lost.

❧

Dear Molly,
I am writing as a fellow Texan who has always agreed with you – at

least, prior to your April 13 column about immigration and high-tech employment. I'm now heading a graduate school of management that serves the Silicon Forest companies of Oregon and southern Washington. The shortage of knowledge workers is a serious matter for them.

At this moment, Intel Corporation, having tapped out the knowledge workforce in Oregon, is opening new sites outside this state. This will mean fewer jobs of all kinds – not just engineering jobs – for Oregonians.

All companies trying to hire qualified people suffer from the shortcomings of American K-12 education, and from the reluctance of young Americans to enter engineering and other technical professions. In recent years, high-tech companies, while generating only a small part of our GNP, have generated most of the new jobs in the U.S. So the visibility of these companies' troubles in hiring knowledge workers is just the way the arithmetic works out. If the automobile industry, say, were a leading job-producer, we would hear instead about their hiring difficulties.

You say the "simple, obvious answer" is "train them." Train whom? People who don't want to be techies? That won't work. People who've been badly prepared by public schooling? That would work, but would take too long. Countries like India and Mexico have prepared, at the expense of Indian and Mexican citizens, fine engineers who now want to work in the U.S., a good deal for us. Needless to say, keeping foreign Ph.D.s out of the U.S. is not going to benefit America's hard-core unemployed. Overall unemployment is about 5% nationwide, but lower (from 2% in Raleigh, NC, to 4% in the Portland-Vancouver area) in the technopolis regions, indicating first that the high-tech firms are ameliorating unemployment, and second that remaining unemployed persons are not located where they are needed.

The root cause of our K-12 education crisis is that Americans don't care enough. I can't think of a better cure than to import people who have shown that they do care about education. If they stay in the U.S., these people will demand the best education for their children, and this will help us all. If history is a guide, the immigrants and their children will become entrepreneurs, starting companies that will produce still more jobs. If they do not stay in the U.S., then they have helped us get past a labor supply crisis. By that time, if we haven't educated or trained U.S. personnel to take the open jobs, it would be our own stupid fault. The high-tech companies have been investing millions in community college programs and in elementary school computer labs to prepare future knowledge workers. Again, it will take time to know which of these programs are efficacious, and to reap the results of the ones that are.

Did you know that half of all H-1B visas go to health care workers? (Computer-related professions account for only 1/4. This information is from *The Oregonian*, April 19, 1998.) There are infinite opportunities to provide human benefit and build wealth through computer-related products and services. It seems Americans who have lived in this country for several generations do not want to be health care workers, and now maybe they won't want to be information workers. If so, I would be disappointed, but there's not much one can do about it.

Making a living as a contract programmer *can* be demeaning and uncertain. If it were otherwise, even more Americans might go for computer careers. And yet, the pay is high for expert programmers and the work is clean and safe. Moreover, the work is here, in the U.S., and not in another country.

The Sierra Club has rejected stricter immigration limits (*Chicago Tribune,* April 26, 1998), so I might tease you about seeming to be in bed with the anti-immigration right. But the *Wall Street Journal* (April 23, 1998), usually knee-jerk reactionary in their opinion pieces, ridicules the H-1B visa system's bureaucracy (and the hell that both American and foreign job-seekers go through under the H-1B process), and comes out in favor of making it easier to bring in foreign knowledge workers. So it is hard to make this out as a liberal-conservative issue.

The Congressional Judiciary Committees are looking at adding 30,000 foreign worker openings in 1999, bringing the total to about 90,000. The fraction of these that are tech workers is a tiny proportion of the estimated 300,000 openings in high-tech companies, and an even smaller fraction of the U.S. unemployed population. Luckily, there is an outside chance American engineering grads can fill most of the rest of the 300,000 positions. By contrast, in Germany the number of open engineering positions now exceeds the annual number of German engineering graduates by a factor of four!

But the engineering graduates are not evenly distributed across the U.S. The economic and political self-determination of places like Portland depends on moving beyond the low-margin, environmentally harmful natural resource exports that have characterized their pasts, and toward higher value-added industries. If this involves bringing in a few educated foreigners who want jobs, well that seems like a win-win, and something not worth getting indignant about.

Sincerely,
Fred Phillips

☯

Subsequently, during the dotcom boom, H-1B quotas were increased. Now the boom has busted, U.S. engineers are out of work, and post-9/11 fears have become part of immigration policy. H-1B visas are being cut back. This is understandable, but it does not vindicate Ms. Ivins' viewpoint. Conscious managers take the detailed view (protection of U.S. jobs) *and* the overview (the health of the economy and the building of international relationships).

Many H-1B professionals' visas been "non-renewed." Their dreams of staying in the U.S. have been dashed. One hopes that they will prosper in their home countries, maintain strong ties with the U.S., and be willing to return here should another chance arise.

Mission

A striking impression can be gathered from the sumiye *school of painting. The spirit of Zen is marvelously expressed. The painting is executed on paper so thin that the slightest hesitancy will cause it to tear. The strokes are swift and decisive. They are final and irrevocable, like a castrated steer. There can be no retouching. The objects are always embodiment of movement depicting the becomingness of nature and the free expression of the intuitive spirit.*

- R.G.H. Siu

A conscious manager reflected on his long practice and how it had changed him. His increased powers of concentration had led to new mental and physical abilities, and vastly better communication and leadership skills. Having followed the path of non-attachment, he faces a pleasant conundrum: What to use his new-found powers for?

He is free to use them for anything at all. Or for nothing at all.

This conscious manager's compassion for others makes the "nothing at all" option unattractive. On the other hand, trying to solve all the world's problems at once, indiscriminately, would dilute his attention and reduce his impact to zero. The conscious manager takes a middle path, committing himself to a well-defined mission.

The next section illustrates the notion of mission, with examples from entrepreneurship, soldiering, and environmentalism.

The last thing IBM needs right now is a vision.
-Lou Gerstner

Verily, oneself is the Eye, the endless Eye.
- The Upanishads

Vision, and Changing the World

"Jinshinkan Dojo" is the name given by my teacher to my aikido school in Oregon. It means "Hall of the Enlightened Mind." "Jin" means enlightened, but also translates as "charismatic." The connection between enlightenment and charisma – a personal presence that allows the conscious manager to connect with people, and excite and influence them – is a key to carefully communicating and implementing the manager's mission. Displaying clarity, focus, and inter-personal sensitivity, the enlightened manager is a charismatic communicator of the vision behind the mission.

A vision describes what the state of things will be when the mission has been completed. At a more particular level, vision also means a picture of how the service or product generated by the mission will fit into the lives of its customers, clients, students, patients, or beneficiaries. The effective manager will devise both an over-arching vision and a particular, customer-level vision. The first, over-arching kind of vision might be "no schoolchild without a hot lunch every day," or Coca-Cola's "world in perfect harmony." The cellular "family plan" – selling multiple cellular phones at a discount to members of a single family – is an instance of a customer-level vision of busy families keeping in touch for convenience, safety, and emotional closeness.

The over-arching vision excites funding agencies, employees, and volunteers. The customer-level vision, if it truly connects with the needs and lifestyles of end-users, inspires investors and clients. Combining both kinds of vision, the conscious manager is able to change the world with new ideas, new products, and new organizations.

Every conscious manager has looked inward to ask, "Should my mission involve changing the world one person at a time, or changing masses of people at once?" Either choice is perfectly okay, but the answer must flow from further introspective questions such as, "Am I attached to a wealthy lifestyle? To a frugal lifestyle? To small projects? Big ones? To privacy? To attention from the media?" The conscious manager, free of attachments, may pursue a mission of any scope and a vision of any scale, acquiring needed skills and helpers along the way.

A manager's enlightened vision accelerates other people's acceptance of his new ideas, or his new presentations of old ideas. Examples from health care and information technology will illustrate these issues of vision. These examples challenge the conscious manager to see the big picture and the small one, and to assemble a total offering that fulfills the beneficiary and the vision.

Why does our healthcare system favor, for example, artificial heart valves (which address a narrowly specific medical problem at great expense) over changes in diet, which can provide inexpensive, systemic improvement in health? The easy answers are:

- Investment will flow to the higher-technology, higher-expense medical regime, and doctors will prefer the heart valve because its installation is highly billable, and reimburseable by insurance.

- Providers have conditioned consumers to take a passive role in the healthcare marketplace.

- Many people don't have the discipline to eat a healthy diet.

- Finally, the patient who is already hospitalized feels a sense of urgency that he did not feel while healthy.

These answers are true only in a broad and superficial sense.

What we now know about change in people and in organizations leads us to a deeper answer. Changing one's diet involves a major change in attitude and behavior. People's resistance to change is so extreme that it is harder to get someone to "be good" than to get them to undergo open-heart surgery.

This seems to conflict with the conventional wisdom of economics. This wisdom says that whoever provides a cheaper, superior solution to a problem will attract the greatest economic returns. Yet, while the heart-valve entrepreneur becomes a millionaire, the dietician and the teacher of stress management usually remain marginal characters in the business world. The model of the master path, as it has been described in this book, resolves this conflict. It tells us that people's attitudes and behavior change after they experience a hunger, an opening event, a practice, support, and tests.

Why is it so hard to persuade people to "be good"? It's simply because there is little or no social reinforcement available to people who are interested in making beneficial changes in their behavior. The purveyor of a high-behavior-change product must also sell the needed social support structure. Alcoholics Anonymous works because its members feel an urgency comparable to that of the acute heart patient. They *know* they need each other, and this sense of urgency is analogous to the "opening experience" of the conscious manager's path. AA's rituals and mutual support mechanisms constitute a practice and a community; refraining from drink is a harsh, ongoing test. Other 12-step programs (for co-dependency, credit card excesses, etc.) modeled after AA have been less successful, because they have not adopted AA's full range of rituals and support practices, or because they were not tightly focused on certain behaviors. Weight Watchers succeeded in its original target market segment by building what amounted to a support group for buyers of its frozen meals, but faltered when trying to expand its clientele to all health-conscious eaters.

Challenges for the organization of the future include globalization, diversity in the workplace, environmental responsibility, and so on. Executives who are actively concerned about these issues gather periodically at roundtables sponsored by WorldTen, The Executive Committee, or other such non-profit and for-profit clubs. Each delicately refrains from calling itself a support group. Bruce Shotkin's Panopolis Foundation in Austin is building an ongoing community (both a physical one and a virtual, computer-networked one) where people can be surrounded by others who are concerned with systemic approaches to health and environment, and where research can be done on how the systemic approaches can be made economically viable.

Ethical entrepreneur Paul Hawkin uses the phrase "failure of imagination" to chide small business people like the dietician and stress management teacher who do not cut a broad swath through their markets. Some of these practitioners, though, are conscious managers who are doing exactly what they want to do, not worrying about the scale of their influence. Others have successfully brought their charisma and enlightenment to bear on building a substantial base of patients and readers; usually, they have included support and reinforcement mechanisms in their service offerings. Still others, not having embarked on a master path, are trying to do good for others, but find themselves frustrated in their ambitions because they have not first worked on themselves.

The conventional wisdom of marketing holds that technology is easily duplicated. Therefore, the conventional wisdom goes, the first entrant must prolong his/her pioneer's advantage by offering superior service, and the late entrant must differentiate his/her product by offering even better service. This is a dangerous half-truth.

Effective entrepreneurs believe their product will change the world. Their technically capable competitors delay entering the market because they do not believe the world is ready for such a product, at least at this price. The conscious entrepreneurs' first-entrant advantage, if he has any at all, lies in the superior force of his vision, in his ability to change the world one customer at a time, or many customers at a time.

Management Challenge: The role of vision. Where does this leave Lou Gerstner, who as IBM's new CEO was roundly criticized for saying IBM didn't need a vision? His full quote was, "There's been a lot of speculation as to when I'm going to deliver a vision. The last thing IBM needs right now is a vision. What IBM needs right now is a series of very tough-minded, market driven, highly effective strategies in each of its businesses." This statement was intended to reassure stockholders that IBM will focus on making money rather than on composing elaborate plan documents. And, in fact, IBM employees have heard and participated in vision discussions since Gerstner's statement, thus keeping them motivated.

How can "each of its businesses" have a strategy without a vision to give shape to IBM's overall strategy? The stockholders and employees are feeling good, but what about IBM's customers? IBM's customers have always looked to Big Blue for technological leadership. They have relied on IBM to sell their companies the most competitive information processing products. Not only that, but they have paid IBM premium prices for these products. IBM's customers pay the premium prices not for the product *per se,* but for the expectation of a steady stream of high-quality future upgrades and service. In other words, a vision that includes staying on the leading technological edge can result in positive brand equity. How can the customers believe IBM will continue to provide the most competitive products if IBM does not have a vision that articulates that goal? Can IBM expect to maintain its high margins if it doesn't formulate and publicize a vision? In the long run, it cannot. In the short run, however, IBM has not ignored user groups and standards committees, making these an essential part of the support structure for IBM's technology customers. The conscious manager, seeing the big picture, understands context. This helps sell the core product and creates more product ideas and selling opportunities. In the examples of this chapter, context meant a social support structure for a core product that required the customer to change his or her behavior.

The compassionate conscious manager may be expected to adopt a mission oriented to alleviating need or suffering. Such a mission implies the conscious manager will be changing people's behavior, whether by teaching, by offering new products and services, or simply by being a good example. That kind of change needs a vision to motivate it, so the mission of a conscious manager who is an entrepreneur – a pioneer of new products, services or ideas – must be accompanied by a vision.

Tool: *Formulating and using a vision.* As a conscious manager, you are an excellent listener and a keen observer. Does your vision resonate with customers and prospects? With investors and employees? Do your vision and mission arouse a passion in you that will allow you to give it one hundred percent? If you answer "no" to any of these, do not hesitate to alter or throw away your vision.

Take a tip from Lou Gerstner of IBM, and put priority on the customer-level vision. An over-arching vision is necessary too, but it is less urgent. Companies are rightly ridiculed when, during sales downturns or stock-price crises, they spend time on high-level vision statements.

Open meetings with a recital of your vision. Put it on advertising material. It helps you stay focused, it keeps your company on track, and it helps your customers understand what you're all about.

We don't have to go to combat to go to war. Life is fired at us like a bullet, and there is no escape...
-George Leonard

Mind of the Warrior

An earlier chapter highlighted Toyoda Sensei's remark that samurai and Buddhist monks of the Shogun era adopted each other's approaches to concentration and commitment. This established the close link between Zen and the way of the warrior. Can that relationship help a budding conscious manager find role models today? To find rigorous tests, and a fitting mission? For some managers, as this chapter will illustrate, the answer is yes.

The chapter will shed further light on the *modus operandi* of the conscious manager – particularly, honing personal skills, controlling organizations loosely, and being focused and steadfast. This discussion of warriors is not all metaphorical; the chapter also explores some implications of these ideas for consciously managing the defense of a nation. The exploration draws on the now-familiar martial arts context, on my experience with the Recruiting Commands of the various services, and on popular films and literature to examine the role of the elite forces and on marketing the All-Volunteer Forces.

In late 1985, twenty-four members of the U.S. Army Special Forces completed a six-month program of daily aikido training under the direction of Richard Heckler and George Leonard. Leonard took the opportunity to look at these students in the context of the popular glorification of the American fighting man: Are the Stallone and Norris movie characters sustainable images of the warrior ideal? Where else might the common man look to find the examples of consciousness-in-action that will serve him in life's battles?

In an *Esquire* article, Leonard reflected that "almost every culture has its own version of an ideal warrior's code." In each version, the warrior evinces self-mastery, self-sacrifice, and extraordinary skills embodying the culture's highest ideals.

Comparing soldiers of this elite military unit to the Japanese samurai and to Don Juan (the Yaqui sorcerer who mentored anthropologist Carlos Castañeda), Leonard found many similarities. The Special Forces students defined a warrior's way as one of "loyalty, patience, intensity, calmness, compassion and will." They agreed that the true warrior "knows himself, knows his limitations." They also agreed in part with Don Juan that the spirit of the warrior is geared not to winning or losing, but only to the struggle. The warrior dedicates himself "to follow his heart, to choose consciously the items that make up his world, to be exquisitely aware of everything around him, to attain total control, then act with total abandon," or as we say in aikido, with *kiai*.

The members of the Special Forces aikido class do not like, glorify or romanticize violence. Yet they have found the military the best place to develop and apply their skills, and the best place to live by the warrior's code. They understand the irony in this, and understand the sad fact that our civilian society in peacetime does not offer the same kind of fulfillment. Why doesn't it? It is possible today to coast through life without experiencing challenge, and many do just that. Disaffected, drug-using teenagers are only the most visible symptom. Adults have the same need to feel truly alive, but can ignore that empty feeling by keeping busy in socially accepted ways. One of life's biggest challenges is to create the challenges that will help us grow.

The warrior exhibits integrity in his actions and control over his life. If the soldiers of the Special Forces follow the warrior path in this sense, how can they reconcile it with being in the military chain of command? They are subject to orders that come down that chain – possibly from an incompetent superior officer – and to court-martial for disobeying orders. Elite units such as the Special Forces (a.k.a. the Green Berets) are political tools, much more so than regular army units. What if an assigned mission is the result of a twisted political motive? What happens to integrity and control in this circumstance?

For the samurai of feudal Japan, bushido reconciled integrity with obedience, to some extent. The samurai had no economic alternative for himself and his family other than military service. Green Berets can apply their considerable skills in civilian life, and very lucratively, if they are so inclined. Don Juan was very much his own man. It's difficult and sort of funny to imagine him taking orders. In the movie *Red Sun,* Toshiro Mifune and Charles Bronson are warriors of East and West. Bronson's character is an outlaw – the perfect free agent, and an interesting contrast to Mifune's, who is constrained by *giri* (duty) and *bushido* (the code of the warrior).

Can U.S. elite forces serve as the warrior ideal in today's society? How can a man or woman maintain a warrior's way of life within the armed forces, given the political and sometimes corrupt nature of the military chain of command?

Elite forces will not be cultural heroes in this country in the foreseeable future. They had that role for a short time in the mid 1960s – remember the song "Green Berets" and the book of the same name? That didn't last long, despite the fact that the Special Forces on the whole operated successfully and honorably in Vietnam, and even now are loyally struggling to aid the Laotian tribespeople who befriended them during the war. Only one thing could propel them back into the popular imagination: a string of dramatic successes combined with continuing media coverage. Even then they would be hard pressed to

104

compete with Rambo, because these movies have tremendous promotional resources and promotional talent at work for them. Sadly, the elite forces won't be allowed even a single success. As we learned from the rescue mission to Iran and the invasion of Grenada, inter-service rivalries and politics ensure that glory accrues to no one.

So much for elite forces as popular heroes. However, there is much that managers can learn from the experience of the elite forces. Leonard found among his Special Forces students a remarkable orientation to service and the protection of society. Further, the elite units are not elite because of their expertise with the complex machinery or managerial functions of modern warfare. On the contrary, their successes in guerilla warfare and counterinsurgency, and their romantic image, are due to qualities of the human mind and body. Using ingenuity, determination and endurance, they are "throwbacks to the pre-technological age of warfare." They develop an unconventional consciousness that reminds me of some aikido and Zen students. Leonard writes of the combat-induced "out of body" experience of one of his soldier friends. After combat experience, elite soldiers develop what one commentator calls "bizarre, inward-looking myths": Moshe Dayan spoke with a young paratrooper who had "become a spiritualist" after many friends had died at his side. He said he spoke with the dead. "Intelligence and sobriety are of no help," the young Israeli soldier said to Dayan, "The borderline between life and death becomes inevitably blurred."

As for the question of military orders in the life of the soldier, the fact is that disobeying an order does not lead inevitably to court-martial. Military men and women clearly remember Leutenant Calley's court-martial for *obeying* orders at the My Lai massacre. The Nuremberg trials are remembered too. The obey/disobey line is a thin one, and treading it is part of the warrior's challenge.

Disobeying orders is almost, among elite troops, the rule rather than the exception. The pressures on these troops are also quite different from the pressures on regular units. Eliot Cohen notes elite units are "more political than regular military forces in the extent to which they capture the interest and imagination of politicians and the public and also in the nature of the tasks they are called upon to perform.... Politicians conduct national security policy with an eye towards persuading the public, and they may [more and more in the future] find light infantry units of this sort useful in trying to do that." Communication technology now allows the whole world to see action at any front, and not incidentally allows politicians to communicate directly with field commanders and to try to call the shots in mid-battle, subverting the lines of command. These considerations politicize the elite units, and inter-service operations and rivalries confuse that line of command. Prior to and during the Iranian mission, according to Arthur Hadley, "Some of the men had not known for months who actually commanded them; nor were they certain from whom they were to take orders." Two of the Navy pilots simply refused to fly.

Confused lines of command, especially in Vietnam, elevated disobeying orders to an art form. Green Berets were known to avoid distasteful tasks by pretending they didn't know from whom they should take orders. This continued a long military history of disobeying orders. Napoleon himself believed that an officer had a right to refuse an order unless his superior was standing beside him as the order was issued. Hadley believes "generals and admirals are the most undisciplined of men. They have succeeded ever since their junior years by bending orders." There are those at the top who are committed to overlooking the behavior of such juniors. A former Army Chief of Staff, when asked what he considered his most important role in that command, replied, "To protect the mavericks." He meant that the methods and events of any future war would be unpredictable. Unorthodox thinkers would be needed to deal with the unpredictable.

One of Leonard's nonmilitary students made the accusation that teaching aikido to soldiers is immoral. George replied that the program had benefited the soldiers in many ways, and in particular had taught them that they could get their way without hitting and bullying. He added, "If we must have soldiers, we should have the very best soldiers we can."

Leonard's reply to the student was philosophically correct but practically irrelevant. The organizational structures and the suspicions separating regular and elite forces – not to mention the relative numbers of the two types of forces – ensure that nothing the elites do will ever have a material impact on regular forces, and thus on the services as a whole. In Vietnam, the regulars never believed in the Special Forces or those who served in them. The sizes of the elite forces are classified information, but it is known that there are fewer than a thousand Navy SEALS. The total number of Americans in uniform is about two million. As elite units are used more and more for small-scale hostilities and antiterrorist actions, they will comprise a greater proportion of the military capability that is actually used – although still an isolated minority in terms of force size.

Historically, despite the use of elite units as laboratories for experimental tactics, few procedures have filtered from these units to the regulars. The martial arts training of elites was and is head and shoulders above that given to regulars. The regulars' training is, in fact, appalling.

In Beirut, the Marine sentries around the building where 241 Marines were killed by a truck bomb stood guard with unloaded weapons. Their commanders felt they were not trained well enough to handle loaded weapons. Prior to 1973, Army recruits received a total of ten hours training in unarmed combat, mostly ineffective blocks, kicks and strikes. In 1973 the Army discontinued this "combatives" (as they called it), mostly for P.R. reasons, to cultivate a more "high-tech" image! Some bases and units still try to sneak in some hand-to-hand training as part of the unit physical training program, but

106

the time available for this is minimal. At Fort Hood, near Austin, troops are exposed to some basic aikido, administered by SportsMind Corporation, the Seattle-based outfit that sponsored Leonard and Heckler's training of the Green Berets.   Also, many soldiers train on their own time at the many dojos surrounding military bases.

Because there is so little time available for training regulars, their unarmed training must consist of simple, direct and powerful techniques that don't require extended practice. There is clearly no scope for innovations to be imported from the highly trained elite units. Striking techniques produce pain and broken bones – if they hit their target – but these won't necessarily stop a man in a kill-or-be-killed situation. For this reason, controlling techniques like those of aikido are a plus for combat training. Some advocate a hard/soft system involving both controls and strikes, like *hapkido*, for regular troops. A soft throwing and controlling practice is important mainly to reduce the lethality of fights *between* U.S. troops, which in peacetime are the majority of a soldier's violent encounters.

Martial arts training is important for all troops. It aids unit morale and cohesiveness. In modern guerilla warfare, the frequent use of infiltration means that rear-area support troops, not just the front lines, are exposed to possible attack and may find themselves in close fighting. But it's unlikely that anything the elite units do or don't do will be relevant to this situation.

To think otherwise is, well, elitist. Most Green Berets come from upwardly mobile middle class backgrounds, just as most of the warriors in historic cultures have come from advantaged classes. Thirty percent of Army Rangers have some college, compared to eleven percent in the regular infantry. The Green Berets have no rank below sergeant. The Navy SEALs now recruit directly from the nonmilitary population, but the entry standards are much higher than for the regular Navy.

Kennedy, Churchill and Dayan all favored the use of elite commandos, and all three like the Japanese samurai, were from the upper crusts of their respective societies. Although the average education of Army recruits is higher than in previous years, there is still a wide educational and "class" gap between elites and regulars that impedes the flow of ideas and techniques between the two groups.

Aikido training will be of some marginal help to the elite forces. What is really needed is more training for the regulars – not just to improve the "quality" of their conduct, but to help them stay alive. The initiative for this will have to come from the regular units themselves. By the mid-1990s, demographic trends reduced the number of high school seniors, the prime recruiting cohort for the armed forces, by a full 25% from its Vietnam-era peak. For the All-Volunteer Force to survive – to avoid a return to the draft – the services must attract recruits by meeting their physical, social, and economic needs. Recruits know they may have to put their lives on the line. To compete with mostly safe civilian jobs, the military must offer the recruit training that will maximize his or her chances of survival. If we must have soldiers, we should have *enough* soldiers.

And a wise manager must know when to wink, when to turn a blind eye, and when to protect the mavericks.

Management Challenge: Finding tests and missions. Until today, Tim worked for a company that had pioneered substantial Internet-based business lines. Two weeks ago he announced his departure to take a job with a pure dotcom that is a "me-too" player in its market space. His new employer's positioning ensures Tim will face greater pressures in his new job, but as he remarked, "For the past year I've only been doing things I already know how to do."

It is clear that Tim is looking for new and better challenges, and wants to increase and hone his skills. At the dotcom, life will be fired at him like a bullet! However, his stated reason for leaving has everything to do with test, and nothing to do with mission. What distinctive mission will be served by working for a firm that is one of many in its market, that is neither the leader nor determined to differentiate itself? Some of Tim's colleagues think that at his age, Tim ought to have a sense of direction. Others believe Tim should be allowed to take his own time growing up. Both groups feel confused by his stated reasons for leaving, and concerned about his prospects for happiness and success in his new position.

Anne, a conscious manager, works in a cubicle near Tim's. She took him aside and told him, "You are sowing confusion and unease around here. If that's your impact here, how are you going to affect people at your new company? If you just want a change and think the grass might be greener there, then tell us that. If you have an idea about what your contribution will be at the dotcom, then tell us *that*. You'll make yourself and us feel better – about you and about our own work."

Tim promised to consider Anne's advice. He spent the weekend examining his own motivations.

On Monday, Tim shared with his longtime colleagues some reasons why his new position will be a better fit with his personality. His new, higher salary, he added, would allow him to contribute more to a charity that is important to his family. He also made some suggestions for redefining his old job description in order to reduce frustrations for his successor.

As a result, Tim's former co-workers remember him fondly and have benefited from the improved work-flow he suggested. His success at looking inward and articulating his motives has served him well at his new employer. Tim now remembers this transition as the start of his own journey toward conscious management.

A flower falls, even though we love it; a weed grows, though we do not love it.
- Dogen

The essence of Zen is that, when you see a turd on the garden path, you pick it up and dispose of it.
- Fumio Toyoda

No More Away

In a recent ruckus over a Texas golf course project, developers tried to launch a canard at the environmentalist opposition. According to this old argument, environmental activism is the shallow, aesthetic pursuit of a few do-gooders who value natural purity over jobs for local workers. Environmentalists, in turn, saw rapacious developers who didn't care about habitat loss and stream pollution on the tract to be developed. The interchange, not really civil enough to be called a dialog, placed participants poles apart on issues of property rights, the heritage of future generations, what taxpayers should have a say about, and what taxpayers should pay for. In this vituperative atmosphere, the conscious manager's job of seeing the adversary's point of view would be a hard one indeed.

We may reasonably expect that conscious managers, even if they do not call themselves environmentalists, will not be indiscriminate polluters. Seeing the big picture, having compassion for others and a sense of consequences and the interconnectedness of things, will prevent a conscious manager from dumping toxins in a neighbor's yard, except in the direst of emergencies. Many conscious managers will adopt environment-oriented missions. They will still appreciate others' need to make a living, even if this is in industries that are not kind to the environment.

When attacked, an aikidoist moves to a common ground before progressing to a peaceful resolution. This action, called *tai sabaki*, is more important than throws and pins, because it places the defender in a position that is at least momentarily safe, offering the option of disengaging or continuing to take the attacker to the ground. It sometimes involves facing the same direction as the attacker, seeing the world for a moment from his viewpoint.

Likewise, in an environmental confrontation, the conscious manager will seek a common ground that serves as a safe base for deciding further actions. The Zen traditions of painting and landscape architecture show the result of the practitioner's awareness of surroundings; to the conscious manager, aesthetics is not a shallow pursuit. It is obvious, though, that a particular aesthetic sensibility will not be the common ground in disputes like the Texas golf course. All environmental issues, however, have implications for public health. Public health is a concern of the majority, and so it can serve as the needed common ground.

After the first Earth Day in 1970, many students graduating with degrees in ecology and related fields found themselves unemployable. Those who repositioned themselves as public health specialists subsequently found jobs. Each of the four main environmental challenges – toxic waste, global climate change, overpopulation, and genetic diversity – has very clear public health implications. Overpopulation strains water and wastewater facilities, leading to the spread of infectious diseases. A species that became extinct yesterday may have secreted a potent anti-cancer compound. Global warming may change crop patterns, endangering the nutritional balance of regional diets.

The commitment of government and industry to public and occupational health provided jobs for these graduates of environmental disciplines. That the grads were qualified for such jobs showed the equivalence of environmental and health issues.

The keys to human health depend on the preservation of nature. Nature's variety is wider than that of the human imagination. Penicillin was first found in a mold organism. Cures for cancer and AIDS are not likely to be synthesized in a laboratory before they are found in the metabolism of a living plant or animal. This is why we strive to preserve this planet as a healthy habitat for man and his companion species.

People understand that effects are not immediately manifested. They may remember Minamata-Shi, Chernobyl, and Thalidomide, where time lags separated the environmental insult and the later onset of radiation sickness or birth defects. The mere possibility of delayed effects turns personal issues into generational issues. Adults may feel they can make informed choices about whether to risk their own health. But just as the bear fights more fiercely when the cubs are at risk, parents become implacable enemies of enterprises that are suspected of poisoning children. This is not aesthetic or economic concern; Love Canal residents were less concerned about jobs than about getting out of town, away from the dioxin-poisoned water supply.

It remains to see how citizens will balance less direct threats to children, e.g. the national debt, bio-diversity, and so on, against jobs. A current test is that of the owls versus the loggers in Oregon. As NAFTA and other trade agreements mature, there will be pressure on our environmental commitment, with free trade bringing in cheap products from nations with less stringent environmental controls. But clearly the aspirations of the middle class cannot be satisfied by gadgets and consumer goods alone.

In a recent poll, 53% of Americans cited environmental problems as the greatest threat to future generations. Various studies show 60%-80% of us are self-described environmentalists. 53% of respondents in a Wall Street

Journal survey have avoided purchasing a product due to environmental fears, and 74% of those polled believe executives should be held personally responsible for their firm's environmental offenses. Americans rank corporate environmental crimes as more serious than insider trading or violations of antitrust or workplace safety regulations. Environmentalism is not a fringe movement; it reflects society's mainstream values. Even polluters have mothers who raised them to clean up their own messes. People who do not learn this lesson, according to Mom, are not fit to join society.

At the time of the first Earth Day, it was believed that environment was a middle-class issue. The rich could buy their own environmental cleanliness, and the poor had more urgent worries. Polluters acted on this. They tried to split the potential opposition by pitting the middle class against the poor and unemployed, and the middle class's environmental aspirations against its own compassion for the poor.

This strategy is unraveling, because even the wealthy are now hard-pressed to isolate their environments from everyone else's. Migrant farm workers organize against toxic pesticide use, and activists agitate to keep dumps and landfills away from low-income neighborhoods. A factory's polluting emissions used to be called "externalities." Implying as it does that waste was placed outside the economic and ecological system, "externality" was one of the most viciously misleading words ever coined by science. Conventional economic theory delayed our coming to realize what Mom always knew: We cannot throw trash away. There is no more "away."

Ordinances banning billboards could be seen as motivated solely by aesthetics. But there is growing evidence that brain development depends on stimuli of fractal complexity, like those provided by trees, mountains, and other natural features. By blocking our view of these features, we are arresting our children's development and forcing mental distress on ourselves. So this is a public health issue too.

Although indoor video-aided golf courses are becoming common, most golfers still prefer strolling through the grassy, tree-lined courses that, according to anthropologists, resemble the African savanna where humans first evolved. How can this be harmful to the environment? Golf courses are heavy users of chemical fertilizers. These, and the partially treated sewage used to water the fairways, run off into nearby streams, making the water unfit for fishing and swimming.

In a democracy, voters are just as entitled to vote their aesthetics as to vote their wallets. But what is dismissed as "aesthetics" is often a citizen's personal assessment of risk, for self or posterity. Subjected to conflicting information from business, government and the media, it's no surprise that citizens become risk-averse. Often, unaided as they are by the expensive public relations advice that the developers' interests enjoy, the citizenry is hard pressed to articulate their feeling of risk in a way that is credible to municipal decision-

113

making bodies. They may lack the sophisticated awareness that decision and risk must be defined in terms of alternatives. Is the alternative to the golf course a shopping mall and parking lot, a grazing pasture, or a wilderness park? Questions of comparative runoff then become different, and probably difficult.

It is ironic, of course, when developers of a beautiful golf course accuse the opposing environmentalists of "aestheticism." Is the spiritual renewal provided by a round of golf on a manicured course greater than that provided by hacking and hiking through the unspoiled wilderness? What national, ethnic, and demographic groups will answer "yes" to this question, and which will answer "no"? Where is the line between aesthetics and religion? Many people feel deeply that the Earth is their mother, or even a part of their own body. Can we distinguish cultural preferences from real public health issues? The British, for example, like their nature manicured, not wild, but are more restrained than Americans about paving it over.

Certainly there are environmental extremists who wish to impose unattainable scenarios of purity, not all of which involve the continued presence of humans on the Earth. Their inability to tolerate human striving and muddling is a neurosis which is quite different from aesthetic concern. A mature and balanced individual is able to tolerate messes – but knows when too much is too much. On the other side of the equation, a mature and balanced individual is able to consider more than the monetary consequences of an action.

In too many communities, acrimony develops between the "real estate rapists" and the "effete environmentalist elitists." In these same communities live people, like the present reader, who are conversant with the environmental science or the principles of risk assessment, planning, negotiation, health, art or anthropology that bear on the dispute. Let us bring our knowledge to bear on informed, constructive community dialog. Despite the complexities, unanswered questions, trade-offs and differing philosophies, public health is a common denominator for everyone's environmental concerns. Using it as a focus, we can work together to design and build a sustainable society.

Fumio Toyoda says that the essence of Zen is that, when you see a turd on the garden path, you pick it up and dispose of it. Would that we could conduct our debate on environment in this clear and straightforward manner.

Recipe

A special transmission outside the scriptures;
No dependence on words and letters;
Direct pointing to the heart of man;
Seeing into one's own nature.
> -Bodhidharma

Before a cookbook can be of use, the reader must have background knowledge. What is a stove? What does "boil" mean? The preceding chapters of *The Conscious Manager* have presented the background concepts for transforming consciousness. The next chapter is a step-by-step guide – a recipe – for this transformation.

Reaching up to a high shelf he took down a square green bottle, the contents of which he poured into a green-gold dish, beautifully carved. Placing this before the Cowardly Lion, who sniffed at it as if he did not like it, the Wizard said: "Drink."

"What is it?" asked the Lion.

"Well," answered Oz, "if it were inside of you, it would be courage. You know, of course, that courage is always inside one; so that this really cannot be called courage until you have swallowed it."

The Lion hesitated no longer, but drank till the dish was empty.

"How do you feel now?" asked Oz.

"Full of courage," replied the Lion.

- L. Frank Baum, *The Wonderful Wizard of Oz.*

How to Become a Conscious Manager

"Well," remarked a local entrepreneur, "the companies I know sure need more conscious management. How can we get it, and quick?"

The need exists, but the remedy won't come quickly. Having more conscious managers will give us well-run companies and public agencies. But there is no instant recipe for improving organizations. It's not as if the president can order up some consciousness software and have it delivered by Fedex! Each manager must start by working on himself or herself. There *is* a recipe for that, though real progress may take years.

Why not jump directly into doing the good deeds we think will improve business and society? We should not embark on crusades before we are qualified, that is, while ego still distorts our motives. Mixed motives produce mixed results. An executive's jumbled feelings of generosity, guilt, and coercion when giving spare change are communicated as clearly as if by telepathy, with the result that the panhandler experiences discomfort and resentment. "Do-gooder" is sometimes a term of derision, for this reason. How much better simply to give, without the emotional baggage.

When asked, "Should I do well by doing good, or do good by doing well?" the conscious manager replies that doing well – as a developed, capable individual – produces good for our organizations and our society. Doing well does not necessarily mean making a six- or seven-figure salary. It does mean developing discipline and enlightenment.

Here, then, is the recipe for preparing a conscious manager – that is, for preparing yourself. Ingredients you will need are: Hunger, an Opening Experience, a Practice, Support, Tests, and a Mission. The cookpot is discipline, and the utensil is perseverance. Add each ingredient in the order shown, and mix.

1. **Hunger**. The preparation begins with a feeling of need, of dissatisfaction with the status quo. The hunger says, "There's got to be more to life than this," "I feel that I could be so much more," or "I want to know why I am here." The reason these are clichés is because few people get beyond this first ingredient. Readers of this book have already felt the requisite longing. So our chapters have emphasized the next ingredients, the first of which is an...

2. ...**Opening Experience**. A moment of meditation, a work of art, a waterfall or sunset, or a passing experience of selfless flow in athletic or job-related teamwork. Any of these can lead to the realization, "Why, yes, there *is* more to life than I thought." This is not always a *transformative* experience; it may be quite fleeting. But it is a brief glimpse into the oneness of things, a reassuring moment without ego. Haven't had one? Don't worry, one is sure to arise from your...

3. ...**Practice**. The Wizard of Oz was half right; the lion already had courage because courage was part of his lion nature. However, Cowardly Lion had strayed from his nature because he had no regular practice. By not giving him one, Oz helped the lion only momentarily.

How often have you heard there is no substitute for practice? How true it is! Only in fantasy can we send the lion directly against the Witch of the West, or, handing Luke Skywalker a new light saber, aim him straight at the Death Star. Only practice can hone skills and reliably open consciousness. Through practice, you will have many opening experiences. You will come to know that these are not miracles, or rather that they are ordinary everyday miracles.

Aikido. Zazen. The management discipline itself. These are among the practices from which you might choose. Other practices are equally valid and useful. Ginny Whitelaw's book *Bodylearning* lists many other possibilities – including gardening – and shows how to choose one that suits you.

It is absolutely necessary, though difficult, to ensure your practice is a path of enlightenment, and not just one of self-indulgence. Modern American marketing has responded with its usual overkill to our need for a spiritual life. Every pursuit, from home decorating to aromatherapy, is now pitched as an easy, painless enlightenment for a low down-payment and a pittance per month. Please compare such pitches against the present recipe, and choose accordingly.

Having a practice often means having a teacher. If you wish to learn something, usually the sensible thing to do is find a teacher and pay for lessons. Zen wisdom about teachers and books being obstacles to enlightenment is a warning, not a hard and fast rule. Be attached neither to the idea of having a teacher, nor to not having a teacher, nor to the question of teacher / no teacher.

A practice is not a formula. You must still bring your personality to your practice, and figure things out for yourself. If your teacher takes all initiative away from you and demands total conformity, you have the wrong teacher. If your teacher demands that you do not indulge your ego – but otherwise allows you and other students to behave variously according to your different natures – then you have the right teacher.

4. **Support**. People you know and trust, and who have the same hunger you do, will give you social support and peer counseling. Your support group may be a sangha (community of fellow seekers), your club, your team, or your board of directors. Be sure your support group are also on a disciplined path. If they are, they will help you persevere through the frustration and despair that are almost inevitable in your journey; if not, they will take you into wasteful or dangerous side trips.

Management Challenge: Finding a support group. One budding conscious manager considered taekwondo as a possible practice. He went to a demonstration of the art, where the students' truculence was obvious. One student lost a tooth in the demonstration, and another broke a finger. Our seeker then investigated the local judo club. He found the members congenial but competitive, focused on the athletics of judo rather than the enlightenment path. Next, he approached an aikido dojo. The aikido students believed in harmony and had built a community that reinforced each individual's feeling of mellowness. Which of these was the best sangha?

None of them! This manager needed to, and did, meet individuals in each of these three martial art communities who were dedicated to the path without ego. The dojo became a place to learn technique and have friends; the informal network of true seekers, cutting across practices, became the sangha.

5. **Test**. Because it is so easy to mistake an indulgent path for a master path, be sure to find a way to face tests. Tests will tell you whether you are following a disciplined master path or just fooling yourself. A test is passed when your teacher says so, when your own sense of integrity says so, and when there are visible benefits to your organization and support group.

"And back to Kansas?" Dorothy asked eagerly. "Well, I'm not sure about Kansas," said Oz, "for I haven't the faintest notion which way it lies. But the first thing to do is to cross the desert, and then it should be easy to find your way home."

Talk about clichés! Everyone from Jesus to Dorothy of Kansas to Carlos Castañeda has had to cross a desert. It is the archetypal test, and usually a metaphor to boot, but no less real and important for all that. Good thing Dorothy – with a lion, a tin woodsman, a dog and a scarecrow – had a versatile support team.

A test is an opportunity to move to the next level. Passing a test shows you are still growing and changing. A test is a gift!

> **6. Mission**. Do not add this ingredient until the other five are thoroughly mixed. At this point, you have developed new personal powers. You are no longer of the conventional world, nor have you become otherworldly; you are in a position to contribute to the well-being of your community in the most effective way possible.

What does it mean to be between worlds in this way? A Zen saying has it that at first a mountain is a mountain; then a mountain is not a mountain; finally a mountain is a mountain again. A beginner on the path sees the mountain the way her family and peers have socialized her to see it. By definition, this is the "conventional" way. Later, after she has experienced some alternative ways of looking at the world, the mountain looks distressingly unlike a mountain. Often this perception comes from getting attached to the idea that the world is an illusion – an idea that is itself neither quite true nor quite false. This is the otherwordly stage, in which the seeker's friends and family say she is in a dream, in the seventh dimension, or a "space cadet." After much more training, the seeker accepts that the mountain is free to be a mountain or not to be a mountain. Now a conscious manager, she feels comfortable in the world of paradox.

Will your mission involve conquering a disease or racial bigotry? Improving quality in manufacturing? Worker re-training? Prison reform? Ending domestic violence? Making a lot of money so you can give it away as you see fit? Something else? Any of these are fine. You will choose a mission without attachment. You will choose a mission that fits your nature. You will pursue the mission with passion but without ego. You will change your mission after you have made your best possible contribution. You and the world will both be better.

Only these six ingredients are needed. But, like menudo or smoked brisket, a conscious manager requires long, slow cooking.

Availability of ingredients
Must you travel to Asia to obtain these ingredients? Of course not! The Journey to the East takes place inside you. To get started, vary your routine in ways that open you to new experiences. Make time for sitting quietly. For additional ingredients and resources, ask trusted friends, search the Internet,

120

look in the yellow pages, and check your bookstore and the "resources" sections of this book.

Variations using local ingredients

Your background – American, Democrat, Catholic, Jewish, Canadian, Quaker, Republican, Japanese, Labor, Protestant, Green, European, etc. – will influence the way you cook from this recipe. This is to be respected. Because of the formative influence of your early home life, it is part of your "nature."

☯

This book is subtitled "Zen for Decision Makers." Why was it necessary to frame conscious management in Buddhist terms? Couldn't we do this in a strictly non-sectarian way? How can a reader combine this interesting and attractive Zen stuff with her or his home tradition? Is the reader, assuming he or she was not raised Buddhist, being urged to become a Buddhist? All these questions deserve serious and detailed answers.

Zen and Zen martial art "feel right" to me and to my students. Zen has a comfortable appeal to people of all backgrounds who question the dogma of their home traditions; in part, this is because Zen does not attempt to replace these with new dogma. A 2001 study showed that it is not money, popularity or luxury that makes people happiest. Instead, feelings of autonomy ("feeling your activities are self-chosen and self-endorsed"), competence ("feeling you are effective in your actions"), relatedness ("a sense of closeness with others"), and self-esteem are the greatest contributors to happiness. It should be clear, at this point in our discussion, that Zen is the clear path to autonomy, competence, and relatedness. The Zen state of non-separation between oneself and the rest of creation is the best self-esteem there is.

And then again, there is the Zen story of the monk who had inherited money and told his abbot he was afraid of growing attached to wealth. "Or to poverty," the abbot added. "Yes," the monk replied, "I understand." "If you understand," said the abbot, "then you might as well be rich." The abbot understood, though, that the richest man is not the one with the most stuff, but the one who needs it least.

So it is not *necessary* to frame conscious management in Zen terms, but to do so is easier, more effective and less dangerous than to try to invent a new secular creed.

The infomercial of a mega-star motivational speaker opens with a customer gushing that she was transformed by his seminar, but couldn't explain to her friends what had affected her so. This is, however inadvertent, an admission of the star motivator's failure. He has built a secular creed, but has given his students no avenue for teaching others, and none for continuing to teach themselves – except, of course, to buy his books and tapes. In great contrast, Zen has a long tradition of teaching methods, many apt parables like the one above, and many teachers. No single teacher is indispensable. This book is only a finger pointing to Zen. You can help others direct themselves to the Zen path, using this book or other pointers. But do not place a pointer – a single book or a single teacher – on an altar and think it is a treasure!

For similar reasons, this book won't offer advice on combining Zen approaches with those of your home tradition. Any such advice risks diluting both traditions, and draws angry letters from purists in each. Readers are encouraged to find their own accommodation in this regard, at a personal level, with the help of their support group, as generations before them have done successfully.

Whether consciousness comes to fruition "in Buddhists, Christians or philosophers," D.T. Suzuki remarked, is immaterial to Zen. There is no need to change religious affiliation to become a conscious manager. Some conscious managers have come to their awareness by the orthodox practice of their home tradition, while rejecting any dogmatism. Others maintain respect for their home tradition and some of its practices while embracing Zen, or another philosophy that attends to both the universal and the particular. Some others formally convert to another creed. In every case, the recipe of this chapter is the basis for their advancement.

All these choices are open to you. Do not regard them as a spiritual smorgasbord, sampling a bit of this practice and some of the other. That would be the path to self-indulgence. Get good advice in advance, sample two or three alternatives, and then, as Jack Palance advised in the movie *City Slickers,* practice One Thing.

I wish you good luck in your quest.

Perspective

The master finished his meal and looked at me. "I hear you want to become a Buddhist. It can be done. We have a special ceremony for this purpose. Quite an impressive ceremony really. All our monks will dress in their best robes. Sutras will be chanted. I'll ask you some questions to which you'll have to answer 'yes.' Then I'll wave my horsehair brush and the sutra chanting will start again and Gi-san will play his drum and the head monk and Ke-san will strike their gong and after that there will be a feast. It can be organized....

"There's something I want to ask. Why do you want this ceremony to take place? Do you think it will do something for you? Do you think you'll get closer to solving your koan?"

I had to admit that I didn't think so. The ceremony was never mentioned again.

- Janwillem Van de Wetering, *The Empty Mirror.*

First become a conscious manager. Then, make conscious decisions. The previous chapter gave the recipe for becoming. The final chapter is about deciding.

At this company, if you want to get fired, say 'That's not my job' or 'Because we've always done it that way.'
- David Learner

Take what you need and leave the rest.
- The Band

Zen for Decision Makers

Q In my MBA program, I was taught to be analytic about decision making. I study alternatives, gather market research, listen to my advisory board, and try to make a decision that balances consensus with the kind of forcefulness that will make me stand out among my peers. If Zen means to act without premeditation, what can it possibly have to do with decision making?

A It will take a whole chapter to answer this very good question.

Attachment

Most people know not to answer "yes" or "no" when asked, "Have you stopped beating your kids?" The question, phrased as a yes-or-no, is a trap. It entices us to go along with the grammar, answer in the affirmative or negative, and boom, the trap closes, leaving us sounding like child-beaters either way. To such an obvious trick question, most people would reply, "I don't answer loaded questions" or "What's bothering *you?*" or "Go to hell."

The Zen koan "What is the sound of one hand clapping?" is exactly the same kind of trap. If we believe the syntax and semantics of the question must shape our answer, we are stuck in paradox – visualizing one hand making a clapping motion, even as we realize there can be no sound without two hands. Our feet are glued to the floor by our *belief* that we should give a straight answer to this question about hands, and by our *attachment* to its grammatical pattern. A student "passes" the koan by transcending this attachment. Strangely, many people regard this transcendence as difficult and mystical, though they would have no trouble at all dealing with "Have you stopped beating your kids?"

When the question is "The XyloCorp contract sounds good; shall we sign it?", the conscious manager does not consider "yes" and "no" to be the entire range of possible answers. The characteristics of the conscious manager suggest a range of responses:

The conscious manager who…	… may answer the question this way:
attends to detail but looks at context; tries to see the big picture	How does XyloCorp fit into our portfolio? Our workload?
doesn't believe everything he or she is told	It sounds good? Who thinks so? What biases could there be in the numbers?
rejects easy labels	What specifically sounds good? What are the downsides?
constantly hones personal skills	I read about a new financial metric we might try to apply before deciding…
is committed to lifelong learning – for everyone in the organization	Did you give the new analysts a shot at this contract?
exercises respect and compassion (but not indulgence) in all dealings	Do the terms give us an advantage and let Xylo save face?
is flexible but not wishy-washy	The team needs to be on board for this to work – have everyone either sign on or sign out by tomorrow noon.
spares no effort to match the right people with the right jobs	Who on our team can work within Xylo's culture?
lets employees put their best foot forward	Pat R. has a knack for communicating with the Xylo crew. Pat's hitting the ceiling at his present post. Put Pat on the Xylo liaison team.
controls the organization loosely	Reassure Xylo we're buying them for their strengths; we won't be stifling them.
gives employees the chance to stretch themselves	Who at Xylo is ready to play in a bigger pond after the acquisition?
tries to see the adversary's point of view	How is this purchase going to be viewed by our competitors? By the Antitrust Division?
shows a creative imagination	This combination could lead to products for the home improvement market, where we've never been before. How can we factor that into the price calculation?
is focused and steadfast in pursuit of a mission	The contract looks good as a stand-alone, but does it move us in the direction we need to go?
uses all the tools at his/her command	How does this feel in your gut? How can we make the press excited about this? What would make our employees rally behind it? Etc….

To decide means to eliminate alternatives. But the conscious manager must first *generate* alternatives. This amounts to being creative and divergent, and it flows from cutting attachments to established responses. After that, it is time to be convergent, to zero in on only one alternative.

Seen in this way, a decision point is not an opportunity to exercise ego. The best decision may be "let Chris decide" or "let's keep an eye on it and see how it plays out." That is, to decide not to decide.

So far, the Zen idea of attachment has proved relevant to decision making. By perceiving and overcoming attachments, a decision maker generates creative alternative actions, makes mission-oriented decisions uncluttered by ego-stroking, and doesn't feel that answers must be shaped by the way a question is asked. In normal conversation, we are not physically pulled by ropes or pushed with sticks. Taking some license with a child's rhyme, we might say:

> Sticks and stones may move my bones,
> But words cannot compel me.

Immediacy and focus

Another part of the question has to do with immediacy and unpremeditated response. How can we eliminate alternatives using strokes that are "swift and decisive, final and irrevocable," making a decision that "focuses infinite experience into instant intuition"?

You can amass substantial (though not infinite) experience through years of practice. This includes your own years on the job, plus the enormous amount that can be learned by talking with peers and mentors, and by reading. A key to internalizing your experience is paying full attention. This oft-repeated Zen advice simply means, eat when you are eating, study when you are studying, walk when you are walking, attend to your interlocutor's reactions when you are conversing. Not paying full attention means being discourteous and easily distracted. A person who is easily distracted is easily manipulated, and cannot develop the depth of character that produces good decisions. Zazen, martial art, and other practices that demand full attention help develop a focus that cannot be distracted.

If this is taken literally, though, a person will focus on one task and continue it for the rest of his or her life! So another key skill is changing your mind. You may say, "Changing my mind is an important skill? Hey, I change my mind dozens of times a day!" But do you change your mind deliberately, or because you are distracted? Do you change your mind instantly and completely from one task to another, or are you overcome by woolgathering and random thoughts before settling on the new task? Try this exercise.

🌀 *Exercise: Changing your mind.* Stand in an open field or a large room. Choose two objects at eye level, 180 degrees apart. Facing one of the objects, stand with one foot in front of the other, as if you were walking and then stopped in mid-step. Focus on the object. Then, pivoting on the balls of your feet, find and focus on the other object. You will find you can do this most smoothly by turning your head first (be very careful not to injure your neck by turning too fast) with the foot-pivot following. Turn back to the first object in the same way, making minor adjustments to your foot position as needed, and repeat.

Put your complete attention on the first object, then put your complete attention on the second object. Do not stop to admire sights between the two objects. Repeat ten times, and do this daily for several days – or make it part of your lifelong practice.

This exercise is central to the study of aiki sword. A defender must give full attention to the swordsman facing him – then, after dispatching him, immediately and completely focus on the swordsman approaching from behind. This is a matter of life and death, and obviously, sightseeing and distraction in the heat of battle won't increase a swordsman's life expectancy.

I asked one master business strategist how he allocates his attention to his many projects. He uses exactly this principle: "I pick one task," he said, "and let everything else slide to hell until I finish it. Then I pick another one..."

Unlike sword cuts and thrusts, most decisions are not irrevocable (the growing branch of management science called "real options" attests to this). But your words when you announce your decisions are irrevocable, so give your utterances your full attention, too!

Zen decisions: What to consider?

Now what about analysis and deliberation in decision-making? Does Zen philosophy encourage recklessness and anti-intellectualism? No. Does Zen condemn thinking, and encourage us to be reactive instead of proactive? No. All the splendid literature and architecture of Zen could hardly have been created, not to mention sustained for two thousand years, by dummies. They were, in fact, created and sustained by people who planned and analyzed. They did not plan and analyze compulsively. They ate when they were eating, swept floors when they were sweeping floors. They made time for planning and analyzing, and during that time, they planned and analyzed. They knew the value of thinking, knew the value of not thinking, and enjoyed both.

Their example is worth following. Make time for planning. Use that time for planning. Then everyday decisions will flow from instant intuition. Ordinarily, much of our hesitation before making a decision is spent calculating our self-interest in the outcome of the decision. When we are clear about the mission and clear about our attachments, we see the big picture and can instantly see the impact of the outcome on everyone in the organization.

The old masters' example is very hard to follow. But when it is followed, the results are wonderful. And luckily, it is not an all-or-nothing proposition. If you can be 20% clearer about your mission and attachments, or 30% clearer 60% of the time, your decisions will be more effective and fulfilling.

What information should inform your decisions? The saying "Zen rejects nothing" means you must not refuse questionable input *a priori*. Be a Zen vacuum cleaner, a Zen swinging door, an ojo de Diós. Accept all data, experience and

128

advice with equanimity. You have faithfully followed the master path; trust your enlightened self to let the useless bits pass through and to let the useful remain. In this way, you bring your finest critical faculties to bear on well-informed, conscious decisions.

Deciding on a mission / deciding on an action

Deciding on a mission is different from making operating decisions within the context of an existing mission. The conscious manager's operating decisions are free-flowing and un-premeditated. But a mission is carefully and deliberately selected. After a meditative shedding of attachments and non-essentials, the conscious manager uncovers his essential personality, the role he is predisposed to play in human affairs. He understands the difference between a predisposition and a compulsion, and *consciously* adopts the mission. He pursues the mission with all the passion, skills, and talents he commands. His decisions cleave like *katsujinken,* the sword that protects life; they flow like a mountain stream.

GLOSSARY
of Japanese and other foreign terms used in this book

aiki   When used alone or as a modifier ("aiki sword") the first syllables of *aikido* describe a mode of action that respects and harmonizes with the energy and unfolding of events. *Aiki* can be contrasted to ways of doing things that go against the flow. *Aiki* does not imply passivity, but rather an alternation of assertiveness and patience that reflects the natural mode of living, growing things.

aikido   A martial art utilizing throws, locks, takedowns, and other non-injurious means of controlling an attacker. An aikidoist defends by blending with the direction of the attacker's incoming energy, then seizing the initiative to throw or neutralize the attacker. Morihei Ueshiba, known as O-Sensei (great teacher), codified the techniques of aikido in the 1920s and continued to refine them until his death in 1969.

bokken   A wooden practice sword.

breakfall   A way of falling that involves slapping the ground or practice mat with the hand and forearm, letting these relatively tough parts of the body absorb kinetic energy that might injure the internal organs were the trunk of the body to hit the ground first.

budo   Martial way. The term means something more than technique or even art (as in martial art); it denotes the ideal life path of a martial artist, encompassing the art (a unified collection of techniques and their rationales) and all its context.

bushido   The *samurai*'s code of honor.

daimyo   A feudal warlord in pre-Meiji Japan, that is, before the 1860s.

dan   Black belt ranks in aikido and other Japanese martial arts.

dojo   Practice hall; place of training in the do (way).

dojo-cho   Head of the dojo, usually the chief instructor.

gaijin   Foreigner, literally "outside person."

gi	Martial art uniform, consisting of loose trousers, tunic, and white, black or colored belt.
Ginza	A section of Tokyo known for shopping and nightclubs.
giri	Duty; obligation.
hanmi hantachi	Defense, while kneeling, against standing attackers. The practice stems from the Japanese sitting posture, called *seiza* (chairs were not in widespread use in pre-20th century Japan), from which the *samurai* must be ready to spring into action instantly.
hapkido	A Korean word, with the same literal meaning as *aikido*. The founder of the art of *hapkido* studied in Japan early in the 20th century under some of the same teachers as Ueshiba O-Sensei, and utilized the principles of blending that characterize aikido, adding also some kicking and punching techniques.
hara	The lower abdomen, where awareness is to be centered in meditation and martial art practice. In particular, a point in the lower abdomen three or four finger-widths below the navel.
hiragana	One of the Japanese systems of writing, consisting of one character for each syllable.
jinshinkan	"Place of the Enlightened Mind." The name bestowed on the Oregon Graduate Institute *dojo* by Shihan Fumio Toyoda, head of the Aikido Association of America.
judo	A system of throws, joint locks, and wrestling-like groundwork. Like aikido, judo places emphasis on using the opponent's balance to his disadvantage. Unlike aikido, judo is most commonly taught as a tournament sport. Its movements tend to be linear, where aikido techniques tend to be circular.
jujitsu	A predecessor of both judo and aikido, jujitsu is a system of throws, locks and chokes. There is little orientation to protecting the opponent, and jujitsu techniques include bone-breaking and other destructive moves.
Kabukicho	A section of Tokyo thick with restaurants and nightclubs.

kanji	A Japanese system of writing that is adapted from Chinese. Each *kanji* character represents a name or an idea, that is, something that would require an entire word in English.
katakana	A Japanese syllabic writing system, like *hiragana,* but used for childrens' instruction, foreign word transliteration, and other special purposes.
katsujinken	"Sword to let live." Using the sword in a disciplined, careful and moral way, under an oath to protect innocent life.
keigo	Inflecting Japanese words to indicate gradations of politeness as one speaks to people of similar and different social rank.
keiretsu	Groups of Japanese companies with extensive cross-ownership. Horizontal keiretsu tie together different industries (usually banking, trading, manufacturing); vertical keiretsu tie manufacturers to suppliers; and distribution keiretsu unify manufacturers with wholesalers and retailers.
kenjutsu	Systems of fencing techniques. Aikido techniques have their historical roots in *kenjutsu* and in *jujitsu.*
kiai	Focusing energy in martial art and other demanding situations. Also, the well-known shout that, in martial art, accompanies the effort to focus.
koan	A conundrum presented for the consideration of a Zen student. Possibly the most famous of koans is "What is the sound of one hand clapping?" To answer successfully, the student must embrace the seeming paradox, transcending the uncomfortably contradictory logic of the koan.
koshi nage	Hip throw, one of a set of throws that levers the attacker over the defender's hip. (Though it sounds backward to say the defender throws the attacker, this is how it works in aikido. Aikido techniques are for defense only. Should an attacker attack by attempting a punch, kick, or grab, the aikidoist defends by means of a throw or one of the other neutralizing moves discussed in this book. An aikidoist never initiates hostilities. Obviously, to practice aikido techniques, each of a pair of aikidoists must take turns pretending to be "hostile.")
kun	One of two main ways of pronouncing a *kanji* character.

kyu	Pre-black belt ranks in aikido and other Japanese martial arts.
mushin	No-mind. Actually, an integrated mind that does not evaluate or judge, but sits in calm expectancy and reacts instantly, on the basis of a total history of stimuli that either have made an impression or have passed through its "swinging door" (see chapter 1) without influencing the mind.
nidan	A second-degree black belt.
randori	Literally, "taking chaos." In aikido practice, this means defending against multiple attackers who are free to attack in any way they please.
romaji	"Rome characters." Systems for transliterating Japanese into the Roman alphabet.
samurai	A knight of feudal Japan, that is, a servant-warrior dedicated to a code of honor.
sandan	A third-degree black belt.
sangha	Sanskrit word for a community of seekers.
satsujinken	Using the sword to destroy life.
sempai	A senior student, especially acting as mentor to a junior student. This is a relative term. If Gloria is a 1st dan, Joe is a 1st kyu, and Sam is a 2nd kyu, then Gloria may be sempai to Joe while Joe is sempai to Sam. In the movie *Rising Sun,* Wesley Snipes addressed Sean Connery (who played an older Japan scholar and a partner in investigation to Snipes' policeman character) as Sempai, while Connery called Snipes *Kohai,* meaning junior student.
sensei	Teacher. Literally, "one who has gone before."
shihan	Teacher of teachers. A person of at least 6th degree black belt rank who has also obtained a shihan's teaching authorization (teaching rank) from the world headquarters of aikido in Tokyo.
shodan	A first-degree black belt. Aikido ranks start with 7th *kyu* (white

belt) and work upward through 1st kyu (brown belt) and onward to *shodan,* black belt. In the black belt ranks, the numbering reverses itself, and higher *dan* ranks have higher numbers.

sokaiya   Bouncers or thugs hired by corporate management to prevent stockholders from having their say at annual meetings.

sutra   Sanskrit word for Buddhist scripture.

taekwondo   Korean martial art emphasizing kicks.

uke   In Japanese martial art, person taking a fall. In aikido this is almost always the attacker (see the explanation under *koshi nage,* above).

ukemi   Falling.

waza   Technique.

yondan   A fourth-degree black belt.

zaibatsu   Pre-World War II Japanese industrial conglomerates, largely family-run. After the war, the Occupation forces replaced family executives with professional managers, and substantially the same company combinations were reborn as the modern *keiretsu.*

zazen   The practice of Zen sitting.

Zen   A movement, associated with Buddhism, that emphasizes simple practices (seated "meditation," chanting, and everyday work) and some more complex pursuits (like martial art and calligraphy), designed to focus the attention and lead to individual enlightenment.

Bibliography and Notes

Introduction

"To achieve a certain kind of thing…" *Bons mots* are often embellished and appropriated, obscuring their true origin. Workman Publishing's *Little Zen Calendar* attributes the opening quote of the Introduction to one Master Ungo, while other sources name Dogen as its originator. Similarly, variations of Nelson Mandela's "fear of our light" epigram (opening this book's "Working for Change" chapter) go back as far as Plato.

"I cannot now imagine my life without the values I have learned from Zen martial art...." And, of course, those taught to me by parents and family. They will understand I'm just trying to keep things simple in this introduction.

People who like the "beat Zen" of Casady and Kerouac will surely misunderstand the title of this book. Beat Zen embraces randomness, nihilism, and casting your fate to the wind; the beat Zen way of decision making would involve rolling dice. Real Zen is about enlightenment, compassion, creativity and discipline.

How To Use This Book

"If you have bought this book you have already passed the Hunger stage of the path." This book's purpose is to further introduce Zen to managers who already feel curious about it or drawn to it. I believe there are very many such managers. The book's contents are tailored to meet their needs. I do not want to risk, via an extended discussion of spiritual hunger, exploiting the longings of other kinds of audiences.

Practice

Two patriarchs are credited with bringing Zen to Japan. Eisai (1131-1215), after studying with Chinese masters, established the Rinzai Zen tradition. In China, Dogen (1200-1253) received transmission of the Soto Zen teachings and returned to teach these in Japan. Among other differences between the two, Rinzai puts greater emphasis on koan training. Both sects survive in Japan and in U.S. schools, dojos, retreats and Zen centers.

Dogen's thought and teachings are summarized in Reiho Masunaga (trans.),

A Primer of Soto Zen: A translation of Dogen's Shobogenzo Zuimonki. East-West Center, University of Hawai'i, Honolulu, ©1971.

A Primer on Zazen

As Shihan Fumio Toyoda has said, martial art is about enlightenment. Aikido students at Jinshinkan Dojo (Oregon Graduate Institute's Aikido Club) sit zazen regularly, for this reason. While Toyoda Sensei speaks of enlightenment in the Buddhist sense, you may find aikido clarifies your relationship with the universe in other ways.

To learn more about zazen posture and procedure in the Rinzai Zen tradition, order the brief handbook published by Chozenji/International Zen Dojo. It is available from the Japanese Cultural Center, 1016 W. Belmont, Chicago IL 60657, phone (773) 525-3141.

Courtesy in Martial Art and Business

"*Dallas Business Journal* editor Glenda Vossburgh uncovered..." Glenda Vossburgh, "Lessons to be Learned from Anger." *Portland Business Journal,* August 27, 1999, page 66. The full Bacon quote is "There is no other way but to meditate, and ruminate well upon the effects of anger, how it troubles man's life And the best time to do this, is to look back upon anger, when the fit is thoroughly over... Whosoever is out of patience, is out of possession of his soul."

"We are angry when we fear..." Just as with anger, the Zen adept and the conscious manager may feel fear but are not attached to their fear. In other words, their fears do not control them. This is an important and a big subject, dealt with admirably for managers in Julian Gresser's book *Piloting Through Chaos.* Gresser's method involves listening to your body. Different parts of your body are sensitive barometers of the fear you feel. By thinking of various aspects of the situation you face, and "listening to your belly" throughout, you can identify what's really bothering you, isolate it, and work on your attachment to it. This method has been used successfully in Julian's many workshops and in his classes at Oregon Graduate Institute. Order his book via www.logosnet.com.

"Anthropologists are beginning to understand how the rank and file can cooperate to undermine harmful power structures..." Vincent Kiernan, "How Egalitarian Societies Rein in Potential Despots." *Chronicle of Higher Education,* December 17, 1999, p. A22.

138

Working for Change

"Alan Watts explained it beautifully." Alan Watts, *The Way of Zen.* Vintage Books, New York, 1957.

"though O-Sensei was not speaking in a Zen context..." "Nevertheless," said D.T. Suzuki, "the teaching and practice of Morihei Ueshiba is at one with that of Mahayana Buddhism, and also the way of Zen." According to William Gleason (*The Spiritual Foundations of Aikido,* Destiny Books, Rochester VT 1995), Prof. Suzuki is quoted thusly in K. Ueshiba, *Aikido Kaiso Ueshiba Morihei Den,* p.235.

"That's my religion. Go get your own." Thanks to Dan Penrod for this Ueshiba quote.

Opening

Martin Buber, *I and Thou.* Scribner's, New York, 1970.

On the Extraordinary

"...what the business writer Adam Smith calls the 'Ballad of the Zen Cowboy.'" Adam Smith, *Powers of Mind.* New York: Random House, 1975. Adam Smith is a pseudonym of a current-day business writer. This book's "Support" section refers to the 18th-century "commercial philosopher" Adam Smith, famous as the originator of modern economics.

The Dignity Debate

"...people want to live and die within their own tradition and cultural matrix." Former Secretary of Health, Education and Welfare Joseph Califano argues against euthanasia in a similar spirit, "You can die...with maximum awareness and...celebrate your mutual dependence" with your loved ones. Joseph A. Califano, Jr., "Here's An Idea: Physician-Assisted Living," ©1999 by *The Washington Post,* appeared in *The Oregonian,* January 4, 1999.

The numbers on membership in managed care come from *Consumer Reports,* October 2001, pp. 27-31. The same article notes 55% of HMO members say they are highly satisfied with their health plan. Fourteen percent of HMO members report having serious illnesses, and of these, 28% report having difficulty getting to see a doctor (vs. 20% of those who were never seriously ill), and 15-22% of seriously ill patients (depending on type of HMO) report having trouble getting needed care, vs. 4-8% of those with no serious health problem.

Richard McCaffery analyzed the Philip Morris-Czech Republic affair for the August 2, 2001 edition of *The Motley Fool* investors' site, http://www.fool.com/news/foth/2001/foth010802.htm.

Support

Charles Hampden-Turner, *Maps of the Mind: Charts and Concepts of the Mind and its Labyrinths.* Collier, New York, 1981.

Zen and Creativity

"In their efforts to pass beyond the intellect, the Zen Buddhists have..." Ralph G.H. Siu, *Tao Of Science: An Essay On Western Knowledge.* MIT Press, 1958.

Sheridan M. Tatsuno, *Created in Japan: From Imitators to World Class Innovators.* Harper Business, 1991.

The *Japan Management Review* reports that Japanese firms are nurturing creativity.... *Japan Management Review* Vol.1, No.1, 1993.

Kao gained a reputation as a leader in innovation and ranks high in *Nikkei Business*'s list of excellent companies... *Japan Management Review,* Vol.1, No.2, 1993. Other studies of Dr. Maruta's approach at Kao include S. Ghashal and C. Butler, "The Kao Corporation: A Case Study" in the *European Management Journal;* an article in *Intersect* magazine, June 1991; and T. Nagase, "Marketing Strategy in a Saturated Market," in an ESOMAR conference proceedings *Marketing, Advertising and Research: Are There East and West?* Amsterdam, 1986.

Test

George Leonard, *Mastery.* Dutton (Penguin Books), New York, 1991.

On Mastery

George Leonard, *Mastery,* op. cit.

So You're Going To Learn Japanese

"I had joined a pilgrimage to the East…" Hermann Hesse, *The Journey to the East.* Farrar, Straus & Giroux, New York, 1968; translation by Hilda Rosner.

"*Mangajin,* a great magazine…" $30/year, P.O. Box 49543, Atlanta, GA, USA 30359.

Thanks to Chigusa Niu for teaching me the phrase "Sannen ni mo…"

Icons and Institutions – Views from Tokyo and Seattle

"What about corporations? As late as 1900, there were only about thirty of them in the United States." This is the number that remained after a wave of mergers and consolidations in the late 19th century.

"Whose interests are those? We Americans are the corporations and they are us." The majority of Americans do not own stocks, and few have employer-funded pension plans. Unfortunately, a financial regime that encourages stock market growth at the expense of GNP growth exacerbates income inequality and is a social lever that gives stockholders a much different set of civic motivations from the remainder of Americans.

"Nowadays people add 'technology' to the list of inputs." As technology is knowledge that resides in people's heads, technology may be seen as a kind of labor. But as people teach each other, knowledge is transferred, and so technology can stick inside a firm even after the original knowledgeable employee departs. This gives rise to the term *intellectual property.*

Much of the WTO debate has involved intellectual property. The compassionate, conscious manager should be aware of the tension between the need to protect innovators' incentives and the prospect of further abuses like the "US trade pressures to discourage developing countries from using provisions that permit compulsory licensing of HIV/AIDS and other essential medicines. This issue, which has been going on for several years and which has been front page news in many foreign countries, has never been addressed in any US stories by the New York Tims, Wall Street Journal, Washington

Post, Associated Press or Reuters before 1999." Newsline, Reuters Health Information, April 1, 1999. "Compulsory licensing of anti-HIV drugs stirs debate in Geneva," by Deborah Mitchell. http://www.ama-assn.org/special/ hiv/newsline/reuters/04015444.htm

A good general information site on MAI is http://www.igc.org/econwg/ MAI/index.html. Other sources consulted in preparing this chapter included:

- Agence France Presse, "Japan's complaint against US at WTO." ©1998 Indian Express Newspapers (Bombay) Ltd., via Net Express <http:// www.expressindia.com>, September 9, 1998.

- Barlow, Maude, "Creeping Corporatism." *The Bulletin.* University of Toronto, February 3, 1998.

- Bremner, Brian, and Irene Kunii, "Japan Special Report – Wanted: A New Economic Model." *Business Week,* November 30, 1998, 63-78.

- Byrnes, Nanette, and Amy Barrett, "Busting up a Balance Sheet Game." *Business Week,* January 11, 1999, p.45.

- *Christian Science Monitor* (1997) http://www.csmonitor.com/durable/ 1997/09/19/opin/opin.4.html.

- Chomsky, Noam, "U.S. Human Rights Policy: Rhetoric and Practice." Transcript of radio talk, Alternative Radio, P.O Box 551, Boulder, CO 80306. 1998.

- Chomsky, Noam, "Multilateral Agreement on Investment." Transcript of radio talk, Alternative Radio, P.O Box 551, Boulder, CO 80306. 1998a.

- Clarke, Tony, "MAI-DAY! The Corporate Rule Treaty." Common Front on the World Trade Organization, Ottawa, Canada, April, 1997.

- *The Economist* (no byline), "Liberalism Lives." January 2, 1999, p. 59-60.

- *The Economist* (no byline), "Profits of Doom." January 2, 1999a, p. 66.

- Feynman, Richard, *The Meaning of It All: Thoughts of a Citizen-Scientist.* Perseus Books, Reading, MA, 1998.

- Hawking, Stephen W., *A Brief History of Time: From the Big Bang to Black Holes.* Bantam Books, 1988.

- Kash, Don E., *Perpetual Innovation.* Basic Books – Harper Collins, 1989.

- Kodama, Fumio, "Technology Fusion and the New R&D." *Harvard Business Review,* July-August, 1992.

- Phillips, Fred (moderator), "The U.S.-Mexico Free Trade Agreement." IC2 Institute Policy Roundtable, University of Texas at Austin, September, 1990.

- Phillips, Fred, "Introduction," in S. El-Badry, H. Lopez-Cepero, and F. Phillips, (eds.), *US-Japan Shared Progress in Technology Management and Technology Policy.* IC2 /JIMT monograph #2, 1994.

- Phillips, Herbert, "Worldwide Standards and Trade: The Players and Their Networks." *APPLIANCE*, October 1998, pp. 72-75.
- Porter, Michael E., "Clusters and the New Economics of Competition." *Harvard Business Review,* November-December, 1998, 77-90.
- Taylor, Chantell, "Rage Against the Machine – the MAI." *Dollars and Sense*, July / August 1998, http://www.infoasis.com/people/stevetwt/WTO_MAI/RageMachine_MAI.html
- Western Governors' Association, http://www.westgov.org/wga/publicat/maiweb.htm, 1998.

"But this has not stopped officials of the European Commission and the Japanese Minstry of International Trade and Industry (MITI) from continuing to speak in favor of the treaty's provisions." MAI in the WTO, http://www.citizen.org/pctrade/mai/WTO/eujapan.htm, Public Citizen / Global Trade Watch, 7 January 1999.

"...the entire press run of the British journal *The Ecologist* was burned..." Harper's Index, *Harper's Magazine,* January, 1999, p. 15.

"It is rare to see a printed criticism…" This assertion is second-hand as regards Japanese-language publications, and based on personal experience with the English-language press in Japan.

"Another writer points out that conservatives..." Lacayo, Richard, "Where the Right Went Wrong." *Time,* December 28, 1998, 107-108.

"As Berkeley economist Bradford De Long says..." Bradford De Long, "Should Money Make the World Go 'Round?" *Chronicle of Higher Education,* December 10, 1999, pp. B4-B6.

An Open Letter to Molly Ivins

"Aiki is not an art to fight with or to defeat an enemy." Morihei Ueshiba in J. Stevens, *Abundant Peace,* Shambhala, Boston, 1987, p.111.

Mission

Ralph G.H. Siu, *Tao Of Science: An Essay On Western Knowledge.* MIT Press, 1958.

Vision, and Changing the World

This chapter is adapted from section 11.1 of Fred Phillips, *Market-Oriented Technology Management: Innovating for Profit in Entrepreneurial Times* (Springer-Verlag, Heidelberg, 2001). Used with permission.

"The conscious manager understands context." Mystery fans will see this in the different styles of Detective Columbo vs. the team of Joe Leaphorn and Jim Chee. Columbo follows one physical clue to another in a linear logic, ignoring context. This is, perhaps, the right way to proceed in Columbo's California, where people are willing and able to reinvent their identities and histories. Tony Hillerman's characters Leaphorn and Chee eliminate suspects and generate new ones using Navajo historical-cultural context and the demands of the Southwestern landscape. These contexts dictate that people are constrained to act in certain ways and not in others.

The most Columbo can do is identify whodunit. Leaphorn and Chee can find solutions that restore harmony to the community – and may or may not involve fingering the evildoer.

The Mind of the Warrior

"In an Esquire article, Leonard reflected..." *Esquire,* July, 1986.

"Carlos Castañeda's mentor Don Juan..." Carlos Castañeda, *The Teachings of Don Juan: A Yaqui Way of Knowledge.* Simon and Schuster, New York, 1970.

"throwbacks to the pre-technological age of warfare." Eliot Cohen, *Commandos and Politicians: Elite Military Units in Modern Democracies.* University Press of America, 1984.

"bizarre, inward-looking myths" Cohen, op cit.

"...some of the men had not known for months who actually commanded them." Arthur T. Hadley, *The Straw Giant : Triumph and Failure, America's Armed Forces.* Random House, 1986.

"In Vietnam, the regulars never believed in the Special Forces or those who served in them. The sizes of the elite forces are classified information. It is known that there are fewer than 1000 Navy SEALS." Hadley, op cit.

"Prior to 1973, Army recruits received 10 hours total training in unarmed combat, mostly ineffective blocks, kicks and strikes." Robert Spear, *Surviving on the Battlefield: A Handbook to Military Martial Arts.* Unique Publications, May 1987.

No More Away

A version of this chapter was originally published as "Public Health and Aesthetics in the Environmental Debate" in *Technological Forecasting & Social Change* 55:2, June, 1997, pp.193-195. It is used here by permission of Elsevier Science.

How to Become a Conscious Manager

Ginny Whitelaw, Ph.D., *Bodylearning.* Perigee, 1998.

"Modern American marketing has responded with its usual overkill to our need for a spiritual life." See for example David Crumm and Alexa Capeloto, "'Spiritual Consumerism' Hits Market." Knight Ridder News Service, *The Oregonian,* May 26, 2001, page D7.

"A 2001 study..." Kennon Sheldon, *Journal of Personality and Social Psychology,* February, 2001.

"...then you might as well be rich." This story, without the second punch line given here, is recounted by Peter Matthiessen in his *Nine-Headed Dragon River,* Shambhala Publications, Inc., Boston, ©1985.

The conscious manager...

... attends to detail but looks at context; tries to see the big picture.

... doesn't believe everything he or she is told.

... rejects easy labels.

... constantly hones personal skills.

... is committed to lifelong learning – for everyone in the organization.

... exercises respect and compassion, but not indulgence, in all dealings.

... is flexible but not wishy-washy.

... spares no effort to match the right people with the right jobs.

... lets employees put their best foot forward.

... controls the organization loosely.

…gives employees the chance to stretch themselves.

... tries to see the adversary's point of view.

... shows a creative imagination.

…is focused and steadfast in pursuit of a mission.

…uses every tool at his or her command.

A Note About the Author

FRED PHILLIPS is an educator and executive who has taught Zen martial art for more than 25 years. As head of the Management department at Oregon Graduate Institute of Science and Technology, he has built the Northwest's most admired management degree program for high technology leaders. He is author of the textbook *Market-Oriented Technology Management: Innovating for Profit in Entrepreneurial Times,* and Associate Editor of the journal *Technological Forecasting & Social Change.* A longtime Texan, Fred now lives in Beaverton, Oregon, with his wife and daughters. He holds fifth-*dan* rank in aikido.